BASEBALL
DRILL BOOK

GORDON GILLESPIE ★ JAMES PETERSON

MASTERS PRESS

A Division of Howard W. Sams & Co.

Published by Masters Press
(A Division of Howard W. Sams)
2647 Waterfront Pkwy E. Dr, Suite 300,
Indianapolis, IN 46214

Credits:

Cover design by Julie Biddle.
Cover photo provided by the Indianapolis Indians.
Diagrams by Julie Biddle, Sara Wright, Terry Varvel and Lisa Barnett.
Text design by Leah Marckel.

Library of Congress Cataloging-in-Publication Data

Gillespie, Gordon, 1926-

    Baseball drill book / Gordon Gillespie and James Peterson.
        p.   cm/ — (Spalding sports library)
    At head of title: Spalding.
    ISBN 0-940279-59-2 : $14.95
    1. Baseball—Training. I. Title II. Series.
GV875.6..G55 1993
796.357—dc20

93-5193
CIP

PREFACE

The Baseball Drill Book has been written for coaches and athletes at all competitive levels. Each of the more than 200 drills was selected for its ability to provide you with an effective learning environment for the fundamental skills and techniques attendant to the great game of baseball.

For organizational purposes, the drills have been placed in one of the three basic groupings according to a player's position, a specific baseball skill, or a particular game situation. Each drill offers baseball coaches a terrific teaching tool for providing their players with the requisite attributes for success. Many of the drills, however, could easily apply to more than one position or involve more than one unique skills. As a result, you should keep an open mind when incorporating these drills into your overall training program. Whenever necessary, you can make adjustments in the method you use for conducting a drill in order to make that particular drill more appropriate for your specific situation.

We believe that the considered use of the drills presented in this book can have a positive impact on the success of your team. Repetition and feed back are two of the key factors which will determine the extent of the effect that these drills will have. As a general rule, the drills are most effective when they are performed regularly as an integral part of your training program. You can enhance the effectiveness of each drill by taking steps to ensure that each participant in a drill is given clear and immediate feedback regarding his performance in the drill.

We believe that *The Baseball Drill Book* will contribute to your efforts to ensure that your team plays to the best of its capabilities.

Play Ball!

ACKNOWLEDGMENTS

We are indebted to several individuals who helped to make this possible. First, we would like to acknowledge the assistance of Masters Press, particularly Tom Bast and Holly Kondras for their ongoing support during all phases of development for this project. We are also grateful to Roseanne Kiesz for her help in preparing the typed manuscript. Finally, we have both been blessed with extraordinary support in all phases of our lives (including this book) from our wives, Joan Gillespie and Sue Peterson.

Baseball Drill Book

Key to Diagrams

Direction of Player	———————➤
Thrown Ball	- - - - - - - - - ➤
Batted Ball	∿∿∿∿➤
Rolled Ball	· · · · · · · · ·➤
Coach	x
Players	○
Target	▦
Catcher	●
Wall or Fence	——————
Base	□
Cones	△

1

DEFENSIVE DRILLS

Infielders

1 READY, SET, GO!

Objective: To develop player reaction time and footwork. To reinforce the mechanics of the proper ready position.

Equipment Needed: None required (although players can use gloves).

Description: Players line up in rows approximately arms distance apart from each other facing the coach. Upon command from the coach, the players assume a ready position – weight on the balls of their feet, prepared to move immediately in any direction. The coach makes necessary corrections and/or adjustments in the ready positions of the players. The coach then blows a short burst on his whistle and points in the direction he wants the players to move. The players instantly sprint five yards in that direction and resume the ready position facing the coach. The coach can either have the players relax before resuming the drill or point in a new direction to continue the drill immediately.

Coaching Points:

- The coach can vary the drill by either requiring the players to use a crossover step when initiating lateral movements or adjusting the length or nature of the required movement.
- This drill may be used as a warm-up exercise.

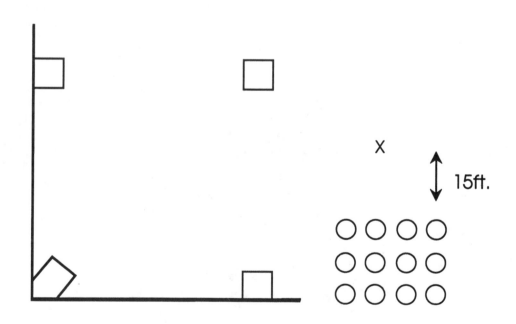

2 CROSSOVER STEP-REACTION DRILL

Objective: To develop footwork (particularly the crossover step), enhance kinesthetic awareness, improve fielding mechanics, and practice throwing skills.

Equipment Needed: Gloves and one baseball per two players.

Description: Working in pairs, the players start on the foul line about 25 feet apart facing each other. The player closest to home plate starts the drill by rolling the ball 10 to 15 feet to the center field side of his partner. Using a crossover step, his partner moves to the ball, fields it, cushions it to his belt and throws it back to the player who started the drill. Both players continue the drill in this fashion until they have moved approximately 150 feet in a straight line toward center field. The players then return to the end of the line, and the drill continues.

Coaching Points:

- Players can vary the type and speed of the rolled (thrown) ball to be fielded.
- Competition can be created by either timing two pairs' repetitions and naming the fastest team the winner or by awarding points for each successfully fielded ball.

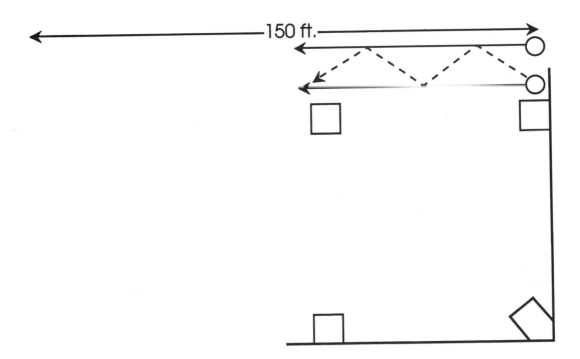

3 FLICK THE BASEBALL

Objective: To develop throwing skills and techniques by emphasizing wrist action and proper ball spin.

Equipment Needed: Gloves and one "50/50" colored baseball per two players.

Description: Working in pairs, players stand facing each other approximately 10 to 12 feet apart. Using a specially colored baseball (half one color, half another), the players flick the ball back and forth to each other, aiming at the receiving player's chest. All velocity on the ball is imparted by means of wrist action. Each time before flicking the ball, a player places his throwing elbow in the glove hand and holds it stationary out in front of the body. This position limits a player to using only his wrist and forearm to "flick" the ball. On each throw (flick), the player should attempt to get maximum spin on the ball and keep the two colors of the ball side-by-side as it moves to his partner.

4 FLUID ARM-ACTION DRILL

Objective: To develop and practice the proper mechanics and techniques of throwing.

Equipment Needed: Gloves and one "50/50" colored baseball per two players.

Description: Working in pairs, the players kneel down on one knee and face each other 40 to 60 feet apart. Using a specially colored baseball (half one color, half another), each player throws a ball to his partner, aiming at the receiving player's chest. Prior to throwing the ball, all players hold the ball by placing their first two fingers side-by-side on either side of the two colors of the ball (the midline) and their thumb exactly on the midline underneath the ball. As they throw the ball, the players should analyze the spin on the ball. If the midline of the two colors of the ball doesn't remain perpendicular to the ground while the ball is in flight, and if the colors don't stay side-by-side during the throw, the player making the throw should review where his fingers were placed on the ball and the position of his wrist while making the throw. While throwing, the wrist, elbow, and shoulder of the throwing arm should be relatively loose and flexible. It should never be tight and rigid. As the throwing arm is moved rearward to initiate the throwing motion, that arm should be fully extended in a non-rigid manner. Then, as the throwing arm is brought around, the flat (palm-side) portion of the wrist is completed by having the wrist flick the ball and the throwing shoulder follow-through.

Coaching Points:

- The coach should require each player to perform a specific number of properly executed throws.
- The coach can vary the drill by adjusting the distance the players kneel from each other.

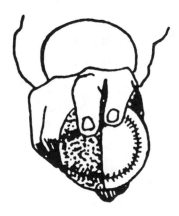

Place fingers
and thumb in
center of ball

5 THROWING FOR ACCURACY

Objective: To improve throwing mechanics and techniques. To develop throwing accuracy.

Equipment Needed: Gloves and one "50/50" colored baseball per two players.

Description: Working in pairs, the players stand 60 to 90 feet apart, facing one another. The drill begins by having a players throw to his partner, using a half-and-half colored baseball. The player attempts to throw the ball to the center of his partner's chest. His partner catches the throw and holds his glove exactly where he caught the ball so that the accuracy of the throw (relative to its position in the chest area) can be readily seen. Points are given to the thrower based upon where the ball is caught: chest = five points, head = three points, legs = one point, and one point is subtracted for any throw away from the receiver's body. A running total of points earned is kept. The first player to earn a predetermined number of points wins the drill competition.

Coaching points:

- Players should analyze the spin one the balls that they throw. On properly held and thrown balls, the two colors will remain on opposite sides and the center division line will remain perpendicular to the ground while the ball is in flight.
- Coaches should analyze the throwing mechanics and techniques of the players and make corrections as appropriate.
- The drill can be varied by having a player throw the ball after fielding a thrown ground ball.

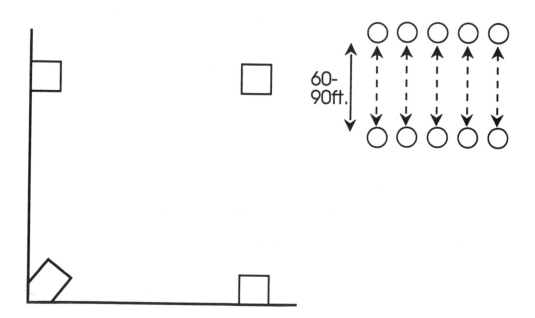

6 EASY RHYTHM

Objective: To enhance the "blending" of the mechanics of fielding into a smooth (coordinated) effort.

Equipment Needed: Gloves and one baseball for every two players.

Description: Working in pairs, the players stand 70 to 90 feet apart facing one another. The drill begins by having one player (A) roll (throw) various types of ground balls to his partner (B). Player B fields the ground ball and, using the skip-and-throw technique throws it back to A. Player B's throw is directed at the chest of A. Player A catches the throw and continues the drill by rolling another ground ball at B. The players switch roles after player B has fielded five balls.

Coaching Points:

- Coaches should make corrections in the fielding and throwing mechanics of the players as appropriate.
- Coaches should emphasize the need to assume a proper ready position before fielding a ground ball and should reinforce the techniques involved in properly moving to a ground ball to field it.

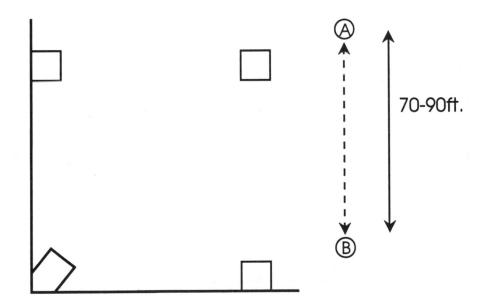

70-90ft.

7 SHORT HOP

Objective: To improve glove action. To practice fielding short hops.

Equipment Needed: Gloves and one baseball for every two players.

Description: Working in pairs, the players stand 30 to 50 feet apart facing one another. The players throw difficult short hops to each other that must be fielded. The degree of difficulty of the drill is enhanced by varying the speed and the direction of the thrown short hop.

Coaching Points:

- Players should focus on the ball from the time it is thrown to a point where it is all the way into the glove which is then cushioned to the fielder's belt.
- Players should be reminded to keep their feet stationary and rely on moving their knees, hips and hands to catch the short hop thrown directly at them.
- Players should backhand short hops which go to the throwing-hand side.
- Competition in this drill can be achieved by awarding points for properly fielded balls and keeping score.

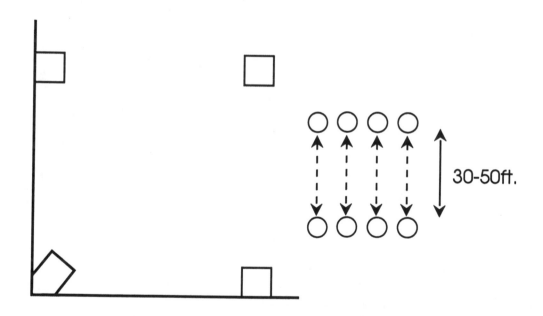

30-50ft.

8 SHORT HOP, PROTECT YOUR GOAL

Objective: To improve glove action and practice fielding short hops in a competitive situation.

Equipment Needed: Gloves, four cones or other markers, and baseballs.

Description: The drill involves competition between two pairs of players. One pair stands in a ''goal-area'' which is approximately ten feet across, facing another pair of players who are in a similarly marked area about 50 feet away. The objective of the drill is to throw a ground ball through the other pair's goal area. The throwing team is awarded a point for each ground ball that gets through the opponent's goal area. The first team to score a predetermined number of points wins the competition.

Coaching Points:

- The entire team can be divided into pairs and competition conducted between all of the pairs.
- The difficulty of the drill can be increased by gradually increasing the width of the goal area which has to be defended.

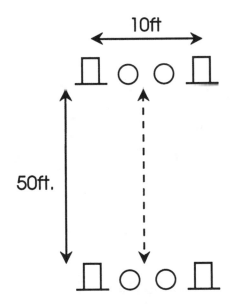

9 BACKHAND FIELDING

Objective: To improve movement mechanics. To practice fielding balls on the throwing-hand side.

Equipment Needed: Gloves and one baseball for every two players.

Description: Working in pairs, the players stand 60 to 75 feet apart facing one another. The drill begins by having one player (A) roll a ground ball to the throwing-hand side of his partner (B). Player B should be forced to backhand the ball. Before each ground ball, the player who will be fielding the ball should assume the proper ready position. As the ground ball is rolled, B should execute a quick crossover step to his throwing-hand side. Upon reaching the ball, player B should firmly plant his throwing foot, go down to the ball by bending his back and legs as appropriate, and put his glove in the proper position to field the ball — open wide and low to the ground. Player B will then focus on the ball until it enters his glove, cushion the ball up and into his waist, and raise up and make a hard, overhand throw to player A without taking a step. Player B should field five ground balls and then switch roles with player A.

Coaching Points: Players fielding the ball should shove off with their throwing-side leg in order to generate sufficient power in their throws. As a rule, the skip-and-throw technique should not be used because it will take too much time to beat most runners.

10 PEPPER

Objective: To develop quickness, throwing skills, fielding techniques, and bat handling ability.

Equipment Needed: Several baseballs, gloves, and a bat.

Description: The drill involves at least two players: one who serves as a hitter (A) and one (or more) who acts as a fielder (B). The two players stand approximately 25 feet apart. The drill begins by having the fielder throw (pitch) the ball to the hitter, who attempts to hit the ball back to the fielder using a shortened, controlled swing. Catching the hit ball, the fielder tosses the ball back to the hitter, and the drill continues in a non-stop fashion for a predetermined amount of time or number of swings. Upon reaching that predetermined point, the players rotate.

Coaching Points:

- Hitters should focus on bat control. One way to accomplish this is to required the hitter to hit the ball to a specific spot relative to the player who threw him the ball (hit to the opposite field).
- Fielders should focus on using the proper techniques for fielding the ball and throwing it quickly and accurately.
- While more than two players can engage in this drill (by increasing the number of fielders involved in the drill at any given time), the extra fielders reduce the amount of fielding that any one player actually gets within a specific period of time.
- Variety can be added to the drill by having the player who fields a ball hit to him, throw the ball to a designated cutoff player instead of back to the hitter.

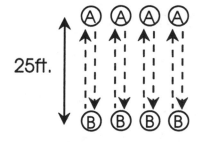

11 DROPPED-BALL FIELDING

Objective: To develop fielding and throwing skills. To enhance quickness.

Equipment needed: One baseball and gloves.

Description: The drill involves two players, using one ball, who are standing approximately 20 to 40 feet apart (depending upon the hypothetical game situation). The drill begins by having a player drop the ball 6 to 8 feet from himself. Once the ball reaches the predetermined distance, the player pounces on the ball, attempts to work on a particular play the he might have on a ground ball during the game (for example, middle infielders might pivot as if they were initiating a double-play, first and third basemen might imagine that they were fielding a bunt), and then throws the ball to his partner. His partner continues the drill by repeating the same sequence of actions. The drill continues for a set period of time or number of plays.

Coaching Points:

- One of the primary keys to the effectiveness of this drill is that the player who drops the ball should explode the ball.
- This drill is an excellent method for warming-up the infielders prior to team infield practice.

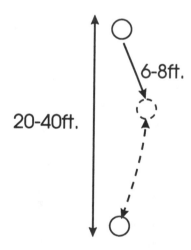

12 WALL BALL

Objective: To improve ball handling skills and improve reaction time.

Equipment: A wall, and one rubber ball and glove per player.

Description: The drill involves one or more players who are standing approximately 20 to 25 feet from the wall. The drill begins by having each player throw a ball against the wall. Each throw is fielded by the player who made the throw. Variety and difficulty are incorporated into the drill by having the player vary the speed, location, and type of throw. The drill continues for a predetermined number of throws or length of time.

Coaching Points:

- The use of proper fielding techniques should be emphasized at all times.
- The closer a player stands to the wall, the greater the emphasis on quickness.

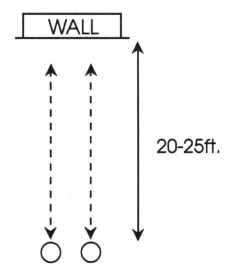

13 LOW THROWS

Objective: To develop the ability to handle low throws and to improve footwork.

Equipment Needed: Gloves, baseballs, and a base.

Description: The drill involves two players standing approximately 30 feet apart. One player is positioned next to a base. The drill begins by having one player throw a ball into the dirt at the other player. That player fields the throw and throws a similar ball back at his partner. Both players concentrate on fielding all types of low throws. The player close to the base tries to keep his foot on the base while fielding the ball as he would during an actual game situation (for example, a first baseman on a low throw, or a middle infielder while fielding a low throw on an attempted steal). After a predetermined number of throws, the players change positions, and the drill continues.

Coaching Points:

- Proper footwork and fielding techniques should be emphasized at all times.
- Variety and difficulty can be incorporated into the drill by varying the speed, location, and type of throw.

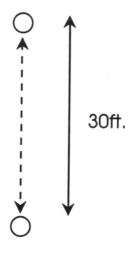

30ft.

14 3-6-3 DOUBLE PLAY

Objective: To enable first basemen and shortstops to develop the skills and techniques involved in making the 3-6-3 double play.

Equipment Needed: Gloves, several baseballs, and bases.

Description: The first basemen (A) and shortstops (B) form two separate lines: one next to first base and one on the shortstop side of second base. The coach (or the next person in the line of first basemen) stands approximately 25 feet from first base on the home plate side. One of the shortstops (C), acting as a baserunner, is being held on first base by a first baseman. The drill begins by having the coach roll a ball to the first baseman which forces him to come off of the base to field the ball. When the ball leaves the coach's hand, the runner takes off for second. The first baseman fields the ball and initiates the 3-6-3 double play. After a preset number of plays, the players rotate to the end of the line or exchange positions.

Coaching Points:

- Variety can be added to the drill by having the coach vary the location, type, and speed of the ball thrown to the first basemen.
- The drill could initially be conducted without a runner actually being held on.
- The drill could also be conducted with the first baseman playing behind the runner.
- If necessary, early in the season, the distance between the bases can be shortened to minimize arm strain.

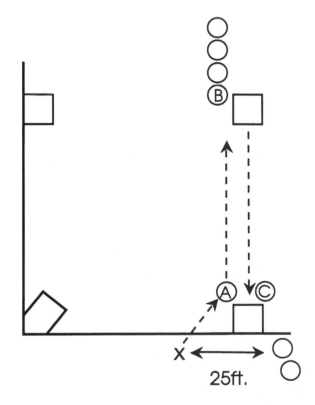

25ft.

15 INFIELDER CUTOFF RELAY DRILL

Objective: To develop the skills and techniques involved in making relay throws quickly and accurately.

Equipment Needed: Gloves and baseballs.

Description: Players perform the drill in groups of three. The drill involves the three players formed up in a straight line approximately 60 feet from each other. The drill begins by having the first player in the line throw the ball to the player in the middle of the line. Already having turned his body to his target (the third player in line), the second player catches the throw and quickly first the ball to the third player. This procedure is designed to simulate the cut-home relay throw. The emphasis should be on both speed and accuracy. After a preset number of throws or minutes, the players should switch positions.

Coaching Points:

- The drill can be varied by placing the three players in a triangle formation instead of a straight line. One player stands near the pitcher's mound, while the other two can be positioned either at first base and second base or at second and third. One player starts the throw by throwing to the player near the mound. After catching the ball, that person has the option of throwing it to the designated base.
- When they're serving as the middle man in a relay, first basemen should learn to catch the ball in the heel of their gloves, not the webbing.
- Relay men should be reminded to turn their bodies toward their targets before making the relay throw.

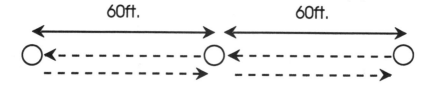

16 SMASH AND FIELD

Objective: To improve the ability to field hard hit balls which are hit directly at an infielder.

Equipment Needed: Fungo bat, gloves, "softie balls", and baseballs.

Description: Players form a single line. Using a fungo bat, the coach (who stands approximately 80 to 90 feet away) hits a hard smash at the first player (an infielder) in line. The player either fields the ball or blocks the ball (if necessary) with his body. If he does not field the ball cleanly, he scrambles after the blocked ball and picks it up as quickly as possible, prepared to make the play.

Coaching Points:

- The drill can be made progressively more difficult by using a "softie" ball initially and then a baseball.
- Other infielders can be incorporated into the drill to give the player fielding the hard hit ball someone to throw to as determined by the coach.
- As appropriate, the coach can increase the speed of the ball he hits by moving closer to the line of players.

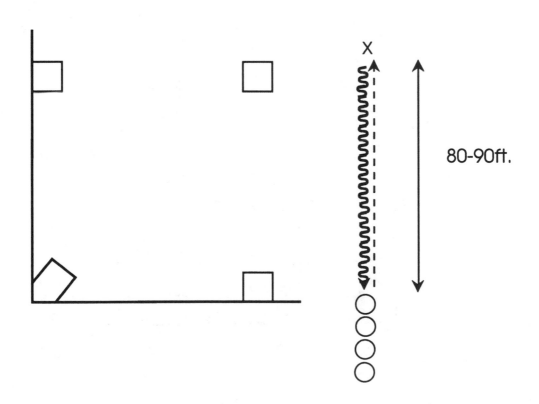

17 SMASH PEPPER

Objective: To improve the ability to field hard hit balls which are hit directly at a player.

Equipment Needed: One set of catching gear for every player in the drill except the batter, a bat, and several baseballs.

Description: The drill involves two or more players in a game of pepper. Every player except the hitter is wearing catcher's gear, or at least shin guards and a mask. One player acts as a hitter, while the others serve as fielders. The batter smashes balls directly at the fielders who are approximately 25 to 30 feet away. The infielders must learn to react to the ball quickly and either field it or block it with their bodies. After a preset number of "hits," the players rotate positions.

Coaching Points:

- The drill can be used to help overcome any existing fear of hard hit balls.
- The drill can also be performed as a triangle drill, one player (A) pitches (from approximately 30 feet), one player (B) hits the ball (pepper-style) to a third player (C) who fields the ball and throws it to A who comes over to cover the base. In this instance, the drill is designed to enhance a player's ability to throw to a moving target. This variation is particularly beneficial when performed by first basemen.

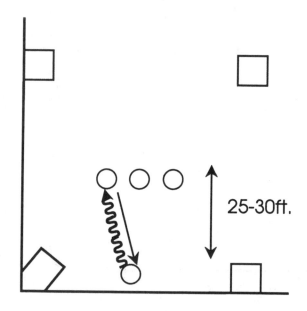

18 POP FLIES

Objective: To develop the skills and techniques involved in fielding pop flies.

Equipment Needed: Fungo bat, gloves, and baseballs.

Description: The drill involves pairs of infielders. Initially, the players throw high pop-ups to each other. One player assumes a ready position and looks straight ahead or down at the ground. His partner throws a high pop-up and yells, "now." The player who must field the ball immediately looks up, locates the ball, moves to it, and catches it. After the players have become relatively adept at this phase of the drill, they progress to hitting fungo pop flies to each other.

Coaching Points:

- If the sun is out, always place the infielder in direct line with the sun, so that he practices shading his eyes and making the play.
- This drill should be performed on all types of days – cold, windy, rainy. (The tougher the weather, the better.)

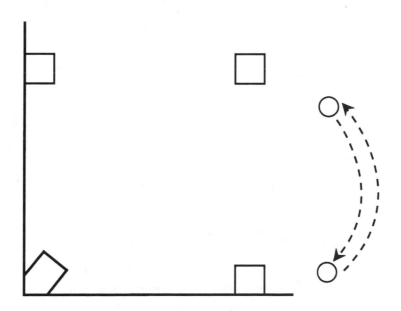

19 CROSS-OVER BASE

Objective: To develop the ability in first basemen to shift to the outside of the bag and tag it while catching a high throw in that direction. To teach the fundamentals involved in shifting, leaving the bag, taking a throw, and tagging a runner.

Equipment Needed: Gloves, baseballs, and a base.

Description: The drill involves two players, at least one of which must be a first basemen. Standing in the infield area approximately 30 feet away, one player throws the ball on the home plate side of first base to the first baseman who adjusts his body position accordingly while either tagging the bag with his foot or a runner with the gloved hand with the ball.

Coaching Points:

- The drill emphasizes good judgement and proper footwork.
- The difficulty of the drill can be increased by varying the type and location of the throw.

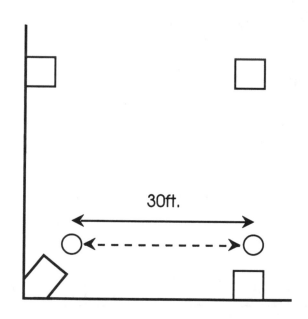

20 THREE PERSON RUNDOWN

Objective: To develop the skills and techniques involved in a rundown play.

Equipment Needed: Gloves, baseballs, and two bases.

Description: The drill involves three players, one acting as a baserunner and two infielders. The coach initiates the drill by throwing the ball to an infielder (A) who is standing next to the base where a baserunner (B) has allowed himself to be picked off. The runner takes off for the next base and attempts to either "steal" the base or avoid the tag as long as possible. The infielder who caught the original throw runs the ball at the baserunner and attempts to force him to continue running toward his partner (C). At the appropriate time, A throws the ball to player C to make the quick tag. After a preset number of rundowns, the players switch positions.

Coaching Points:

- Tagging the runner out as quickly as possible is emphasized.
- A second baserunner and another infielder can be added to make the drill more difficult.

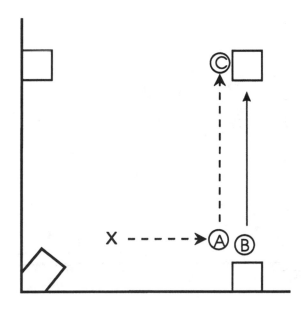

21 THIRD STRIKE THROW TO FIRST

Objective: To teach first basemen the proper way to set up to receive a throw from the catcher on a dropped third strike.

Equipment Needed: Gloves, baseballs, and a base.

Description: The catcher rolls a ball five to ten feet away from himself, retrieves the ball, and attempts to throw out a phantom runner at first base. The first baseman sets up on the coaches box side of the bag and gives a glove target to the catcher. The first baseman always attempts to give the catcher a good angle to throw at, so that a batter would not be hit in the back by the throw.

Coaching Points:

- The drill could be progressively modified to include an actual baserunner once the basic retrieving-throwing-catching skills are mastered.
- The difficulty of the drill could be increased by having someone other than the catcher roll the ball to be retrieved by the catcher. The location of the throw should then be varied so that the catcher is forced to react to the ball.

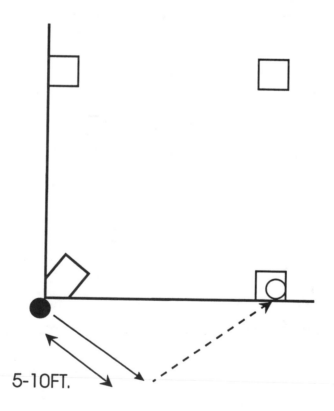

5-10FT.

22 BETWEEN INNINGS

Objective: To have the infielders work on fielding techniques and throwing accuracy.

Equipment Needed: Gloves, baseballs, and one base.

Description: The drill involves five players: a first baseman (A), a shortstop (B), a second baseman (C) , a third baseman (D), and an extra infielder (E) (preferably another first baseman). Between innings of a game, the first baseman works the bag and takes throws from the shortstop and the third baseman. At the same time, the extra infielder, assuming a position about 15 feet up the right field line, takes throws from the second baseman. Both the first baseman and the extra infielder concentrate on throwing relatively difficult-to-handle ground balls so that the infielders can work on their fielding skills. Each infielder should attempt to field at least five balls and make five accurate throws between each inning.

Coaching Points:

- Carelessness should not be tolerated.
- All infielders should focus on utilizing proper fielding techniques and making an accurate throw each time they field the ball.
- The first baseman should concentrate on improving his fielding skills and using proper footwork.

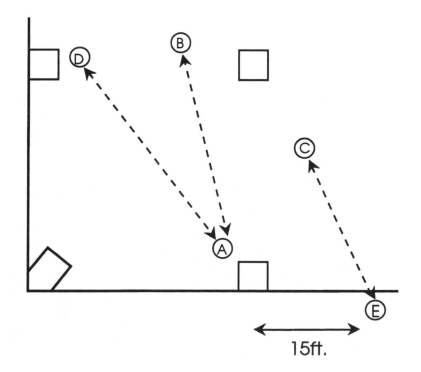

15ft.

23 PADDLE GLOVE BALL

Objective: To improve an infielder's ability to use two hands while fielding a ball. To develop an infielder's ability to get his body into the proper position while fielding a ball.

Equipment Needed: Baseballs, a first baseman's mitt for the first baseman, and paddle gloves for the infielders. (A paddle glove is a piece of ¾ inch plywood shaped somewhat like a glove with straps running through the wood which allows the athlete to hold onto the wood and use it like a glove.)

Description: The drill involves a coach hitting or throwing ground balls to two infielders who are wearing paddle gloves. Using two hands, the infielder fields the ball and throws it to the first baseman.

Coaching Points:

- Infielders should be encouraged to get their bodies behind the ball (assume a position where the ball is centered in the middle of their bodies while it is being fielded) and to use two hands while catching the ball.
- Paddle gloves can also be used by two infielders while simply playing catch.

24 KNEE WALL/FENCE CATCH

Objective: To practice using a short arm delivery while throwing.

Equipment Needed: Gloves, baseballs, and a wall or fence.

Description: The infielders pair-up. One player (A) kneels with the soles of his feet and his back pressed against a wall or fence. His body is erect. His partner (B) is standing approximately 25 to 30 feet away. Player A initiates the drill by rotating his upper body to throw the ball to B. During the rotation, his hand will hit the wall, forcing him to shorten his backward rotation and throw the ball from "his ear." Player B catches the ball and throws it back to A. After a predetermined number of throws, the players rotate positions.

Coaching Points:

- Players should concentrate on getting zip on their throws from a kneeling position.
- All throws from a kneeling position should be made quickly.
- The difficulty of the drill can be increased by moving the non- kneeling partner farther away.
- This drill is particularly beneficial for catchers who are having trouble mastering a short arm throwing delivery.

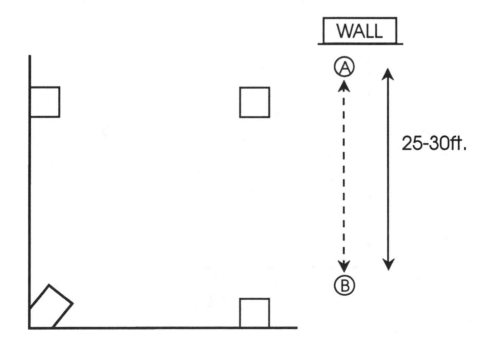

25 THROWING FROM THE RELEASE POINT

Objective: To practice throwing the ball from the proper release point. To improve fielding techniques.

Equipment Needed: Gloves and baseballs.

Description: A coach hits or throws a ground ball to an infielder. The infielder fields the ball, brings his hand to the proper release point (ear-level) and throws it to the first baseman (A). No matter where the grounder is fielded in relation to the player's body, the player is required to then raise his body and throw the ball from the proper release point.

Coaching Points:

- Players should be reminded that when they alter their release point, they increase the likelihood of having a throwing error.

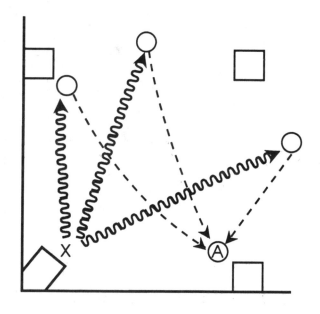

26 THE FIRST-AND-THIRD, READ-THE-RUNNER DOUBLE STEAL

Objective: To improve the communication between the third baseman and the catcher on a first-and-third double steal situation. To practice the techniques involved in having the catcher attempt to throw out a runner at third base.

Equipment Needed: Gloves, baseballs, and bases.

Description: The drill initially involves the catcher and the third baseman. The drill begins when the catcher who has the ball looks at third baseman during a hypothetical first-and-third double steal situation. The third baseman is responsible for determining whether the runner at third base has ventured too far down the line during the attempted double steal. If the third baseman feels that the runner has gone too far, he throws his hands in the air which is the signal for the catcher to throw to third base. The third baseman moves to the base, sets up three feet inside the bag, gives a knee-high glove target to the catcher, takes the throw from the catcher, and quickly tags the runner who is coming back to the bag. As the drill progresses, a runner at third base can be incorporated into the drill. Subsequently, a runner at first could also be added to the drill to conduct the first-and-third double situation "live."

Coaching Points:

- The catcher should fake towards second base before firing to third base.
- The catcher should concentrate on throwing to the glove target. Carelessness may result in the runner being hit in the back.

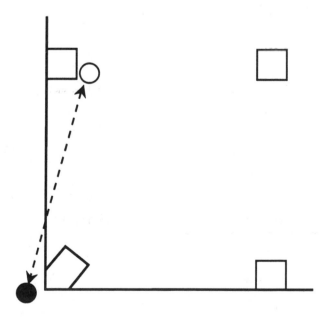

27 BAD HOP

Objective: To practice fielding bad hop grounders. To develop "soft" hands.

Equipment Needed: Gloves and baseballs.

Description: Players divide into pairs. Each player stands facing his partner who is approximately 15 feet away. The drill involves having each player (A) alternately toss a bad hop grounder to his partner (B). The partner fields the ball and attempts to throw a bad hop grounder back to A. The drill continues for a preset number of bad hop grounders being fielded by each player or a preset length of time.

Coaching Points:

- Players should be encouraged to make their throws difficult to field.
- Competition could be conducted between the two players on the basis of fewest misses.
- The drill could also involve practicing tagging an incoming runner. For example, after fielding the bad hop grounder, the player could be required to execute a swipe tag (to simulate tagging an incoming baserunner).

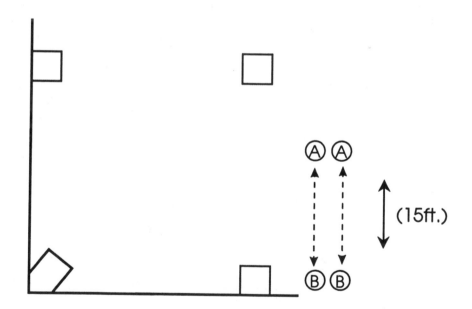

28 DOUBLE PLAY PIVOTS

Objective: To practice double play pivots and throws.

Equipment Needed: Gloves, baseballs, and a fungo bat.

Description: The drill involves all of the infielders. The drill begins by having a coach who is standing approximately 30 to 40 feet in front of home plate in the middle of the diamond hit or throw a ground ball to a left side infielder (C). The infielder fields the ball and throws it to the second baseman (B) to start the double play. The second baseman makes the pivot and relays the ball to first base (A). After a preset number of plays or length of time, the coach can initiate the drill by hitting or throwing a ground ball to a right-side infielder. The drill continues for a predetermined length of time.

Coaching Points:

- If the throwing arms of the infielders get tired early in the season, the distance between the bases can be shortened for the drill.
- Proper fielding and throwing techniques should be emphasized at all times.

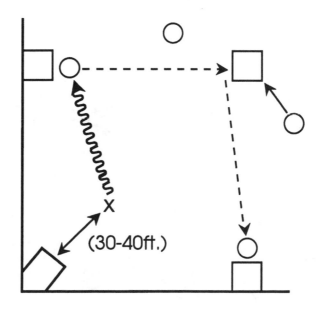

29 PIVOT AND HURDLE THE DUMMY

Objective: To teach middle infielders (shortstops and second basemen) to avoid a sliding runner as they complete the double play.

Equipment Needed: Gloves, baseballs, bases, and a football blocking dummy.

Description: The drill involves having the second basemen (C) and shortstops (B) line up in two separate lines. The shortstops are required to toss the ball (simulating the start of a double play relay) to the first second basemen . That player catches the toss, tags second base, makes the pivot, and relays the ball to first base (A). As the ball is tossed to the player who must then relay it to first base, the coach rolls a blocking dummy at the feet of that player. That player must learn to skip over the dummy as he makes the throw. After each play, the dummy is retrieved by the coach, and the drill continues with the next player in line. After every player in a line has had the opportunity to practice this skill a preset number of times, the two lines switch responsibilities (the tossers become the double play relay throwers and vice-versa).

Coaching Points:

- The player relaying the ball to first must get his shoulders and body turned toward first base as he is throwing in order to minimize his chances of being injured if a collision with the baserunner occurs.

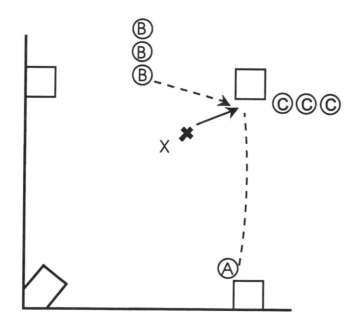

30 RUN THROUGH

Objective: To practice fielding a slowly hit ball and throwing out the runner at first base.

Equipment Needed: Gloves, baseballs, and a fungo bat.

Description: Using a fungo bat, a coach continuously hits slow rollers toward the infielders (third basemen, shortstops, and second basemen). The infielders charge the ball, scoop it into their gloves, and throw out the runner at first base. The drill continues for a preset length of time or number of balls fielded.

Coaching Points:

- Infielders should be reminded to keep their heads down and look the ball into their gloves while fielding.
- The ball should be played with both hands, unless it has almost stopped. In the latter case, the infielder can play it with his bare hand.

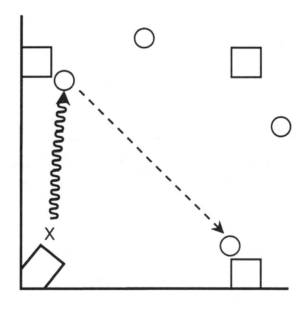

31 PROPER RELAYS

Objective: To teach middle infielders the skills and techniques involved in being an effective relay man.

Equipment Needed: Gloves and baseballs.

Description: The drill involves three infielders in a line, approximately 60 to 70 feet apart from each other. The player in the middle (B) is preferably either a shortstop or a second baseman. Both players on the end of the line (A and C) are facing the middle player. The drill begins by having player A throw the ball to B who is acting as the relay man. Player B catches the ball and relays it to C. Both player A and C simulate tag plays whenever they receive a relay from B. After a preset number of relay throws by B, the three players switch positions.

Coaching Points:

- Players should concentrate on using proper throwing techniques.
- Players serving as the relay man should face the player throwing him the ball, catch the ball, and then turn and strongly fire the ball to the target.

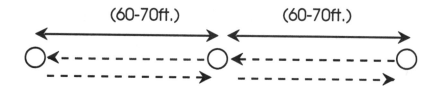

(60-70ft.)   (60-70ft.)

32 1-4-3 DOUBLE PLAY

Objective: To practice the techniques and footwork involved in a double play which is started by the pitcher.

Equipment Needed: Gloves and baseballs.

Description: The drill involves three players: the pitcher, the second baseman, and the first baseman. The drill begins by having the pitcher drop a ball at his feet. At that point, the second baseman breaks for the base. The pitcher then quickly picks up the ball and fires it to the second baseman who makes the proper pivot and throws the ball to first base to complete the double play.

Coaching Points:

- The focus is on having both the pitcher and the second baseman make strong, accurate throws and having the second baseman use the proper footwork when making the double play pivot.
- Once the basic techniques of the 1-4-3 double play have been mastered, the drill can be made more difficult by either adding a runner at first base or having a coach hit grounders to the pitcher to start the double play.

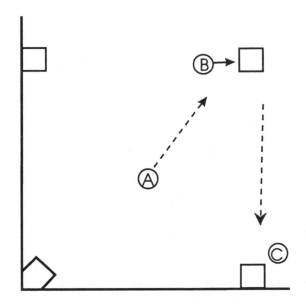

33 FORCE AND TAG PLAYS AT HOME

Objective: To enable infielders to practice fielding ground balls from a drawn-in infield position and throwing out runners at the plate.

Equipment Needed: Gloves, baseballs, and a fungo bat.

Description: The drill involves as many infielders as the coach chooses to use (preferably a full complement of infielders). The infielders assume a position on the lip of the grass. Using a fungo bat, the coach hits ground balls to the infielders who are then required to throw out an imaginary runner at home. The coach calls out the situation, either a "force play" or a "tag play."

Coaching Points:

- On force plays, the infielder should throw a chest-high strike to the catcher. On a tag play, a knee high throw to the catcher is required.
- The emphasis is on using proper fielding techniques and making quick, strong, and accurate throws.

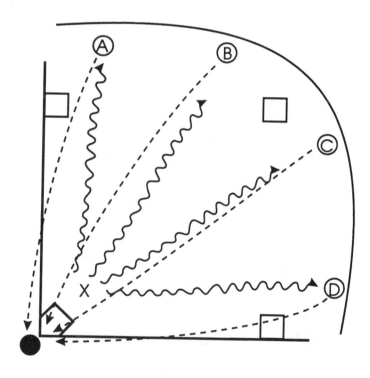

34 SIDE-TO-SIDE

Objective: To develop lateral quickness. To practice fielding techniques while moving laterally.

Equipment Needed: Gloves and baseballs.

Description: The drill involves having the infielders work in pairs. The two players stand approximately 20 feet apart facing each other. One player (A) acts on the hitter, while the other player serves as the fielder (B). The drill begins by having player A roll the ball to B's right or left. Player B moves laterally to field the ball and feigns a throw to a designated base on every ground ball he fields. Player A varies both the location and the relative difficulty of the ground ball he throws to B. Player A tries to get B to extend as far as he can to work on forehand and backhand plays.

Coaching Points:

- The difficulty of the drill can be progressively increased by having the infielder actually throw the ball to first base or by having player A hit grounders (using a fungo bat) to B instead of throwing them.

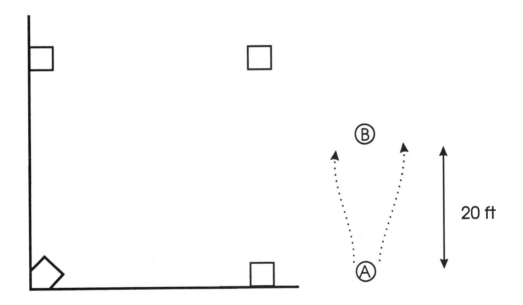

35 POP UP AND UP

Objective: To practice fielding pop flies.

Equipment Needed: Gloves, baseballs, and a fungo bat.

Description: The drill involves as many infielders as the coach chooses to use (preferably a full complement of infielders). The drill entails having a coach hit fungo pop flies to various locations and having the infielders practice fielding the pop-ups. The pop flies are hit to each of the locations the infielders might have to deal with during the game: short left field, short center field, short right field, on the infield, and in foul territory.

Coaching Points:

- More than one fungo hitter can be used at a time to increase the number of pop flies which must be handled.
- Whenever possible, the drill should be performed on a sunny day to enable the infielder to practice not losing the ball in the sun.

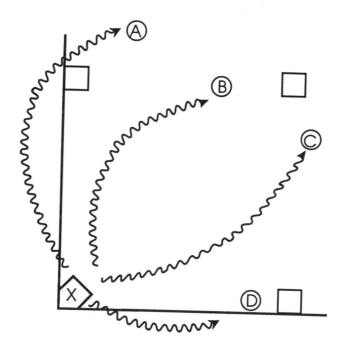

36 FIRST AND THIRD

Objective: To practice defending against the first-and-third, no-out situation. To provide an indoor activity during inclement weather.

Equipment Needed: Gloves, moveable rubber bases, tennis balls, and a bat.

Description: The drill involves two teams of infielders with six infielders per team: catcher, pitcher, first baseman, second baseman, third baseman, and shortstop. Catchers wear a mask. The game is played with a tennis ball. Team 1 takes the field. Team 2 positions runners at first and third and has a batter at the plate. The tactical situation is runners at first and third with no outs. The catcher (or the coach) serves as the umpire. The batter must use a choke grip while swinging. The batter is given two strikes to advance the runners. He may not walk or receive a base as a result of being hit by the pitch. In addition, he is out if he hits the ball over the infield or fouls off a pitch when he already has one strike. He can bunt, take a first strike, or foul off a first strike. If he makes contact with the ball and hits a grounder, the situation is live. The batter runs to first base and the baserunners attempt to advance. If the batter makes an out, the next player in line becomes the hitter. After three outs, the teams change sides: Team 2 takes the field, and Team 1 is at the plate. The team that scores the most runs wins.

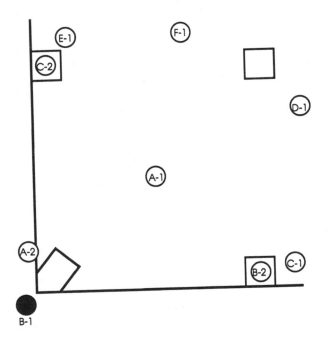

37 DOUBLE UP

Objective: To practice fielding and throwing techniques. To provide an indoor activity during inclement weather.

Equipment Needed: Gloves, moveable rubber bases, and tennis balls.

Description: The players participating in the drill form two lines: one line of fielders and one line of baserunners. A moveable rubber base is set up approximately 70 feet from a gymnasium wall. The baserunners line up next to the wall. The first baserunner stands facing the base with his rear foot against the wall. Adjacent to each other, the first two fielders in line stand facing the wall approximately 60 to 70 feet from the wall. The coach assumes a position between the two fielders. The drill begins by having the coach toss the ball against the wall and yelling the command, "Go." On the command, the baserunner breaks for the base. The fielder closest to the ball as it comes off the wall fields the ball and tosses it to the other fielder who moves to cover the base. The purpose of the baserunner is to simulate "live" action. He is not allowed to slide or crash into the fielder covering the base. After the play, the players rotate.

Coaching Points:

- The emphasis is on proper foot-work and split-second timing.
- The complexity of the drill can be increased by having the fielder covering the base take the throw, pivot, and throw to another base (target).

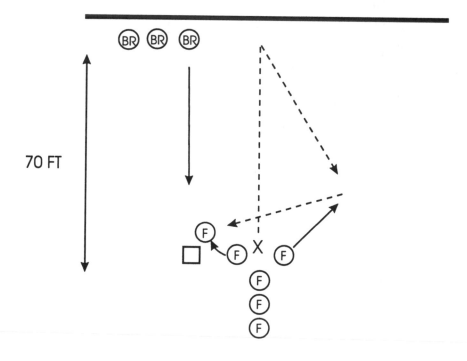

38 POP-THE-TARGET

Objective: To practice the techniques and skills involved in fielding a ball while on the run and making a strong accurate throw to first base. To provide an indoor activity during inclement weather.

Equipment Needed: Gloves, a moveable rubber base, and tennis balls.

Description: A target area, measuring three-by-one foot, is taped on a gymnasium wall approximately three feet above the floor. The drill involves three players at a time and a coach who stands to one side of the target area and judges all thrown balls. A rubber base is placed about 100 feet in front of the wall to serve as a point of reference. One player (A) assumes a position adjacent to the base, approximately 50 feet to the right of the target. A second player (B) stands (out of the line of the throw) next to the target area and retrieves balls thrown at the target. A third player (C), standing 50 to 60 feet in front of A, is responsible for rolling ground balls to A which he must field. Player C can either roll the ball or throw a slow bouncing ground ball. Player A must charge the ball, field it, get set, and throw at the target area as quickly as possible. Points are awarded to player A on how well he fields and throws the ball: three points for a cleanly fielded ball throw inside the target area, two points for a cleanly fielded ball which hits the edge of the target, one point for a cleanly fielded ball which misses the target, and no points for a misfielded ball.

Coaching Points:

- Players should stay low while fielding and keep their eyes on the ball.
- Players should be reminded of the need to set before throwing. Throws made off plays performed in one swooping motion are often wild.
- Point competition between players can be conducted with this drill.

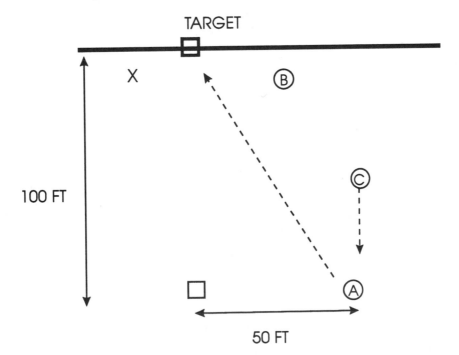

2

DEFENSIVE DRILLS

Outfielders

39 ON YOUR TOES

Objective: To develop the ability to pick up the flight of the ball. To teach outfielders to keep their heads up when running for a fly ball.

Equipment Needed: Baseballs and gloves.

Description: The outfielders line up outside the right foul line facing the infield. On command from the coach, the first player in line sprints to his right and catches a ball thrown by his coach. He then runs back to his left to catch another ball thrown by the coach. Next, he immediately sprints to his right again to catch a third ball thrown by his coach. After catching each thrown ball, the player tosses it back to the coach. After the third ball is thrown (and caught), the player returns to the end of the line. The next player in line steps up, and the drill continues.

Coaching Points:

- Players should run on their toes, not on their heels.
- Players should select and focus on a head-high point while running before they turn to look for a thrown ball.
- Players should look for a thrown ball by turning their heads, not their entire bodies.

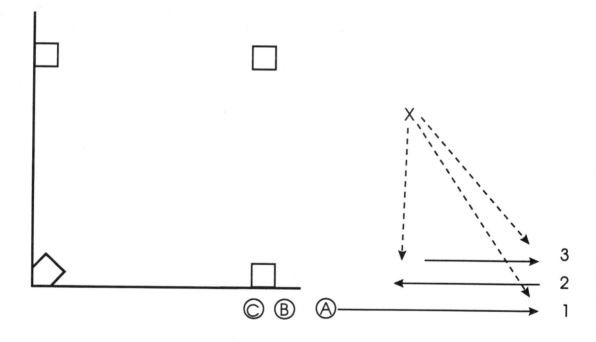

40 CATCH IT IF YOU CAN

Objective: To develop and improve fielding techniques and fundamentals of out-fielding.

Equipment Needed: Baseball, gloves, and a bat.

Description: The drill involves a coach who hits a variety of ground balls and fly balls to players who are positioned in the outfield. In addition, one player is designated as a cutoff (relay) player. After fielding a ball hit by the coach, the player catching the ball throws it to the relay man, who in turn throws it to a player who is serving as a catcher to feed balls to the coach (as needed). Standing on the right field foul line approximately 25 to 30 feet beyond first base, the coach hits balls on a fairly continuous basis. After fielding a ball, the outfielder immediately assumes the ready position again. Once an outfielder has fielded a specific number of balls, a new outfielder rotates into the drill. The player being replaced then either goes to the end of the line or substitutes for either the relay man or the catcher.

Coaching Points:

- The drill can be performed with one or more outfielders at a time.
- The coach can vary the location, speed, and type of ball hit.
- Players should be required to make good throws to the cutoff man.

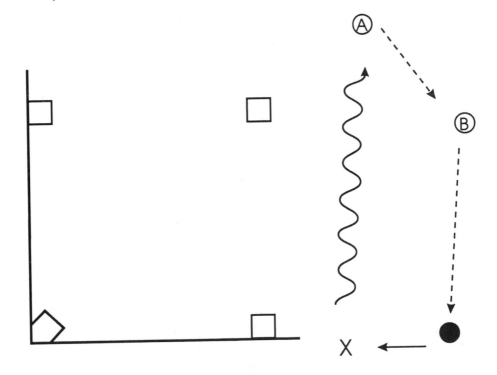

41 BALLS AT THE FENCE

Objective: To develop the skills and techniques required to play a ball which is lying next to a fence.

Equipment Needed: Four baseballs per threesome, gloves, and a fence.

Description: The drill involves three players, two of whom act as outfielders, while one serves as a cutoff (relay) man. Four balls are placed next to a fence about five feet apart from each other. The two outfielders line up about 25 feet from the fence, while the cutoff man is approximately 75 feet from the fence. The drill commences by having the first man in line sprint to one of the balls and pick it up. Right-handed outfielders should pick up the ball with their right foot positioned to the right of the ball without straddling the ball. Left-handed outfielders should position themselves with the left foot to the left of the ball. Upon picking up the ball, a player should begin his throw as quickly as possible at precisely the point where he picked up the ball. After throwing the ball to the cutoff man, the player returns to the starting area. The second outfielder then continues the drill by running to pick up the next ball. After the four balls have been picked up and thrown, the players rotate, and the drill starts over.

Coaching Points:

- Players should be reminded that because the average runner takes four to five strides per second, time is of the essence when initiating a throw.
- More than one group of outfielders can perform the drill simultaneously.

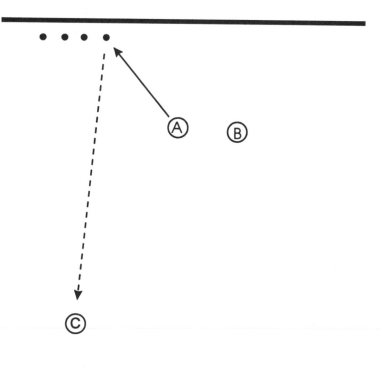

42 FIVE PLAYER RELAY

Objective: To develop the skills and techniques required to make relay throws quickly and precisely.

Equipment Needed: Baseballs and gloves.

Description: Players work in groups of five. Depending on the age of the players, the players line up in relatively straight lines, approximately 60 to 70 feet apart from each other. The drill begins by having the first player in line make a strong, accurate throw to the second player. The second player then makes a similar throw to the third player, and so forth. Once the ball has been thrown to the last player in line, the drill is repeated in the opposite direction. All players should be taught to adjust their body positions while the ball is in flight so that they are able to simply catch the ball and throw it immediately with maximum velocity and accuracy regardless of the thrown ball's path as it approaches them.

Coaching Points:

- The proper techniques for throwing should be emphasized.
- Each cycle of the drill can be timed to set a standard of relative comparison.
- Competition can be staged against two or more groups performing the drill simultaneously.

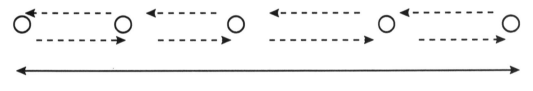

250 FT

43 EVER LONGER CATCH

Objective: To develop arm strength for throwing and to practice long, accurate throws.

Equipment Needed: Baseballs and gloves.

Description: Working in pairs, the outfielders start approximately 75 feet apart and gradually increase the distance between each other to 150 feet. Beginning at 75 feet and continuing every five feet or so, the players throw the ball to each other. The emphasis is on making a long, accurate throw. The ball should be thrown chest high to a player's partner. To get his body's momentum and force behind his throw, a player should crow hop before releasing the ball.

Coaching Points:

- To add variety to the drill, a player could intentionally drop the ball in front of himself after catching it and then scramble after it, before making a return throw to his partner.
- The distance between the players can be decreased if any of several factors suggest that such an action would be appropriate: it's early in the season, the players involved are relatively young, or if one of the players has a sore arm.

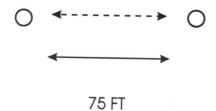

75 FT

44 FIELD LIKE A SHORTSTOP

Objective: To practice fielding ground balls. To improve the ability of an outfielder to throw accurately to a base.

Equipment Needed: Gloves and baseballs.

Description: Working in pairs, the outfielders stand approximately 120 feet apart. One player, serving as a first baseman (A), rolls (throws) the ball to his partner (B). Player B charges the ground ball, fields it like a shortstop, and makes a strong, accurate throw to A (who is hypothetically covering first base). After a preset number of fielding chances, the players switch roles.

Coaching Points:

- Using proper fielding techniques and making a strong, accurate throw should be emphasized.
- Outfielders should be reminded of their need to be able to field ground balls well and to be able to quickly throw to a specific target.

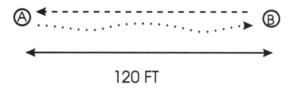

120 FT

45 BODY BLOCK GROUND BALLS

Objective: To practice using the body to block ground balls. To teach outfielders not to let bad hop grounders get by them in the outfield. To improve the ability to scramble after a ball which has been blocked.

Equipment Needed: Gloves and baseballs.

Description: Working in pairs, the outfielders stand 60 to 70 feet apart. The drill involves having one player (A) throw a hard ground ball at his partner (B). Player B moves to the ball, gets in front of it, drops his throwing side knee to the ground, protects his groin area with his glove hand, and uses his body to block the ball to keep it from getting past him. Once the ball has been blocked, player B quickly picks it up and uses his kneeling leg to vault him into a standing position. Player B then makes a strong, accurate throw to A. After a preset number of repetitions, the players switch roles.

Coaching Points:

- The drills can be made more difficult by varying the location and speed of the ground balls which are thrown by player A.
- The need to get squarely in front of balls to be blocked should be emphasized.

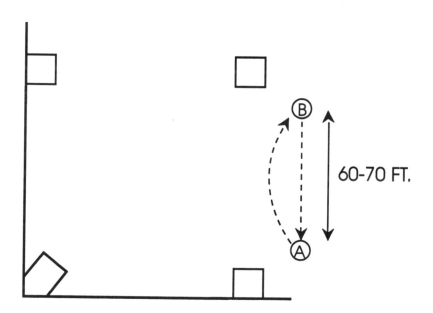

46 CUTOFF RELAY

Objective: To practice hitting the cutoff man with a strong, chest-high throw.

Equipment Needed: Gloves and baseballs.

Description: Working in pairs, the outfielders stand approximately 100 feet apart. Player A flips the ball behind himself, turns and races for the ball, picks it up, wheels to his glove-hand side, and throws a chest-high strike to his partner (B). Player B catches the ball and continues the drill by performing the actions of A in the same order. The drill continues for a preset number of repetitions.

Coaching Points:

- The emphasis should be on quickly getting to and picking up the ball and making a strong, accurate throw.
- Variety (and an increased level of difficulty) can be added to the drill by having either a third player or the coach flip the ball to be picked up instead of player A. In that instance, player A must also learn to locate the ball quickly.

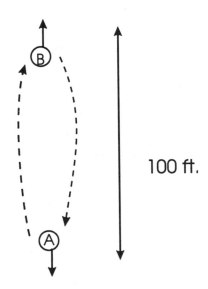

47 SLIDING CATCHES

Objective: To practice catching a fly ball while sliding. To develop the ability to make low or shoestring catches.

Equipment Needed: Gloves and baseballs.

Description: The drill can be performed either outdoors on the outfield grass or indoors in the gymnasium. Long pants should be worn by those players participating in the drill. Working in pairs, the outfielders line up approximately 60 to 70 feet from each other. One player (A) lobs a short fly ball to his partner (B), who races in, slides feet first toward the infield, and attempts to catch the ball on the fly alongside his body while sliding. After a preset number of repetitions, the players switch roles.

Coaching Points:

- Players must learn to accurately judge the flight of the ball and to time their slide accordingly.
- Players should focus on the ball at all times.
- The difficulty of the drill can be increased by varying the location and speed of the lobbed fly ball or by moving the outfielders further apart to make the distance player B must cover greater.

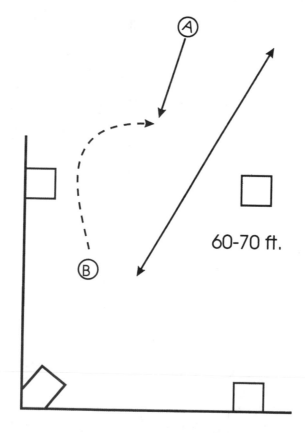

60-70 ft.

48 IN THE ALLEY

Objective: To teach outfielders to coordinate responsibilities on ground balls and fly balls that are hit between them in the alleys (gaps).

Equipment Needed: Gloves and baseballs.

Description: The drill involves two players and a coach. (Note: A third player could perform the duties of the coach in this drill.) One player (A) is positioned in center field, while the other player (B) serves as the flank (right fielder or left fielder) outfielder. The coach throws or hits a ball between players A and B, who must then coordinate who should make the play. The general rule of thumb on all balls hit into the gap, ground or fly balls, is that the flank outfielder will pass in front of the center fielder in making the play. As a result, flank outfielders usually will play line drives hit in the alley which are above waist high because they are passing in front. Center fielders, on the other hand, make the plays on low catches because they are taking a deeper angle to the ball. On high fly balls hit in the gap, the center fielder usually calls off the flank outfielder. In this instance, an exception is made if it is a throwing play and the flank outfielder has a stronger throwing arm.

Coaching Points:

*   The drill can be expanded to include both flank outfielders and the center fielder at the same time.
*   Players fielding the ball initially lob the ball back to the coach. Once the basic skills of the drill have been mastered, the fielder can be required to make a strong throw to a specific target.

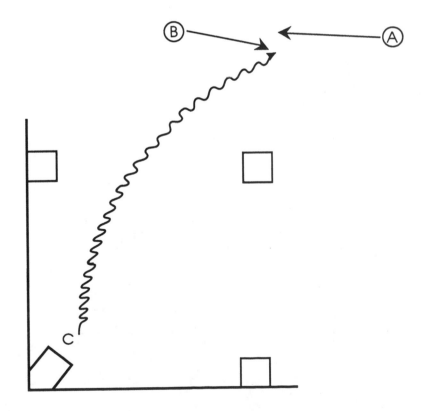

49 COORDINATING POP-UPS

Objective: To enable outfielders and infielders to practice coordinating their "calls" and responsibilities on pop flies that are hit between the two groups.

Equipment Needed: Fungo bat, gloves, and baseballs.

Description: The drill involves a preselected group of players: the right side of play (the first baseman, the second baseman, and the right fielder), the left side (the third baseman, the shortstop, and the left fielder), or the middle of the playing area (the shortstop, the second baseman, and the center fielder). The drill is initiated by having a fungo hitter hit pop flies into the short outfield area. The players participating in the drill are then responsible for coordinating between themselves regarding who must make the play. The outfielder has the priority on the "call" and must make a decision no later than his fourth stride as to whether he is going to take the play of call an infielder onto the ball. Priority rules for coordinating on "tweener" pop flies must be established and followed.

Coaching Points:

- The key is the incoming outfielder reaching a decision as early as possible and yelling, "I've got it" or "you've got it."
- An early call by the outfielder can help prevent a collision (and the resulting injuries) between players.

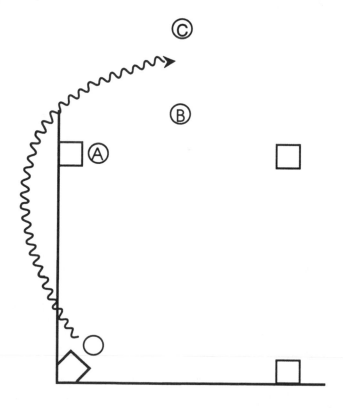

50 FLIP THE SUNGLASSES

Objective: To practice catching the ball under sunny conditions. To teach outfielders how to properly use their sunglasses.

Equipment Needed: Gloves, baseballs, and sunglasses.

Description: Working in pairs, the outfielders stand approximately 50 to 60 feet apart. The drill involves having one player (A) throw a high pop up to his partner (B). Once the ball is in the air, player B works on flipping his sunglasses down, shading his eyes with his glove, and catching the fly ball. After each catch, the players switch roles.

Coaching Points:

- The key for a player is to keep his eyes on the ball at all times. He does not want to lose the ball in the sun.
- This drill can also be practiced indoors. A bright, direct ceiling light can serve as the sun.

51 OFF THE WALL

Objective: To practice playing balls which have been hit close to or off the outfield fence. To develop a "feel" for the fence (wall).

Equipment Needed: Gloves, baseballs, and a fungo bat.

Description: Initially, the drill involves having a coach hit fungo fly balls next to the fence. The outfielders (one at a time) race back and try to make the proper play. They key for an outfielder is to always get to the fence as quickly as he can, find it by feeling for it with his throwing hand, and prepare to make the play with his glove hand. Once the outfielders have mastered the basic techniques involved in the drill to this point, the coach can then expand the drill by hitting the ball against the fence in addition to adjacent to the fence. Whenever this occurs, the outfielders should play the ball off the fence and be prepared to throw the ball to the relay man.

Coaching Points:

- The coach should vary the location and type of ball he hits.
- The drill can also involve more than one outfielder at a time so that they can also work on coordinating the balls hit to or near the fence in the gap.

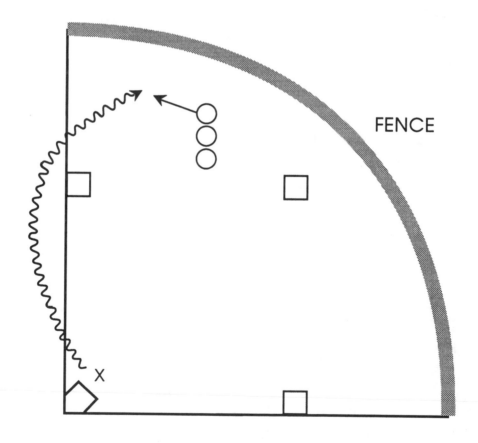

52 ONE LOOK IS ENOUGH

Objection: To develop the ability in an outfielder to hear the crack of the ball on the bat, take one, look, race to the point where he thinks the ball will be, and make the catch.

Equipment Needed: Gloves, baseballs, and a fungo bat.

Description: The drill involves a fungo hitter and an outfielder. The fungo hitter calls out "ready" to the outfielder. Upon hearing the "ready" call, the outfielder resumes his outfield stance and looks at the ground. The fungo hitter then hits the ball. As soon as the outfielder hears the ball hit the bat, he gets one quick look at find the ball. He must then race to the spot where he thinks the ball will come down and make the play. Several stations (each with one hitter and one outfielder) can perform the drill simultaneously.

Coaching Points:

- The fungo hitter should vary the location and type of ball hit.
- The outfielder is only allowed "one brief look."

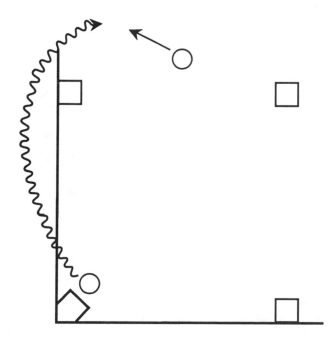

53 LINE DRIVE

Objective: To practice fielding line drives. To improve an outfielder's ability to properly judge line drives which are hit directly at him.

Equipment Needed: Gloves, baseballs, and a fungo bat.

Description: The drill involves one to three outfielders who are required to field line drives which are hit directly at them by the coach. Using a fungo bat, the coach hits a continuous series of head-high drives at the outfielders who must judge the ball and make the play. The outfielders are positioned 150 to 175 feet from the fungo hitter.

Coaching Points:

- Outfielders must learn to judge whether a line drive will sink, sail, or break to the left or right.
- The coach should vary the location and the type of line drives he hits.

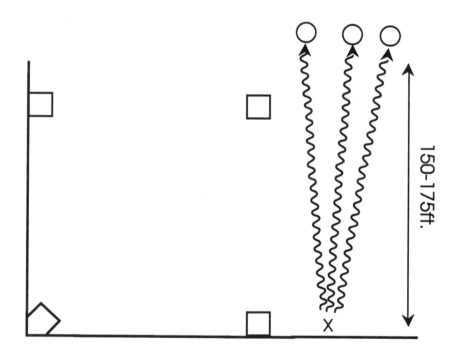

54 ONE-HOP THROWS

Objective: To practice making accurate, single-bounce throws to the bases.

Equipment Needed: Baseballs, gloves, bases, and a fungo bat.

Description: The drill involves having the coach hit fungo fly balls to outfielders who are in a deep outfield position. The outfielders field the ball and then make a strong, one-hop throw to the base designated by the coach (initially second base, then third base, and finally home plate). The outfielders concentrate on making accurate single-bounce, line drive throws.

Coaching Points:

- Competition between the outfielders can be conducted by awarding points for the accuracy of the throw: two points for a one-bounce accurate throw and one point for an accurate throw which either doesn't bounce before getting to the base or bounces more than once, and no points for an inaccurate throw.
- To add variety to the drill, the fungo hitter can vary the location and the type of ball hit to the outfielders; baserunners could also be employed in the drill to simulate "live" action.

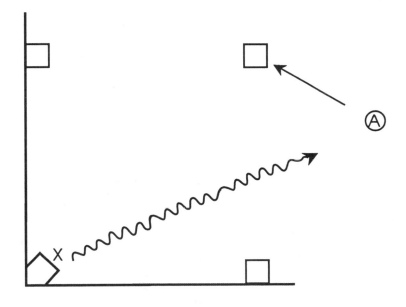

55 FOCUS ON THE CROSS SEAM

Objective: To practice throwing using a cross seam grip.

Equipment Needed: Gloves and baseballs.

Description: Working in pairs, the outfielders start the drill by standing facing each other approximately 60 feet apart. They take turns throwing to each other using a cross seam grip. They should apply the cross seam grip without looking at the ball and should concentrate on completely following through on each throw. The drill continues by having the partners slowly move apart by stepping backward. Every few steps, they throw to each other. Once they have reached a point where they are approximately 150 feet apart, they make one-bounce throws to each other. Still using a cross seam grip, each player throws the ball approximately 10 feet in front of his partner. A cross seam grip will ensure that the ball will follow a direct path in flight and after bouncing. Once the players are approximately 250 feet apart, either the drill can be started over or a third player can be added to serve as a cutoff man.

Coaching Points:

- All throws should be free of sideward motion.
- A cross seam grip will prevent a ball from curving, twisting, or sliding.

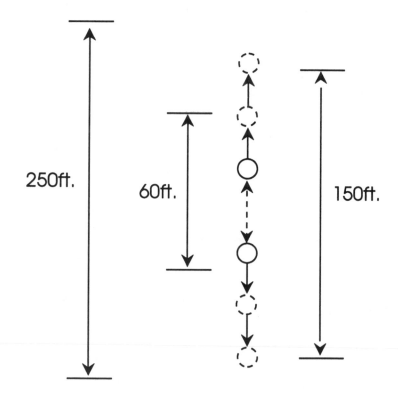

56 MOVING UP

Objective: To practice catching a fly ball while running forward. To develop stamina.

Equipment Needed: Gloves and baseballs.

Description: The drill involves outfielders working in pairs. One player (A) acts as a tosser, while his partner (B) is the fielder. Both players start the drill by standing facing each other approximately 90 feet apart. Player A initiates the drill by tossing a fly ball approximately 75 feet to B who must run up to catch the ball. After catching or retrieving the ball, player B throws the ball back to A and then sprints back to his original position. The drill continues in the same sequence with player A tossing the ball to B. Each subsequent toss, however, is shorter to require player B to run further and faster each time. Once the toss is only about 15 feet, the players switch roles.

Coaching Points:

- Player B should assume a proper ready stance before each tossed ball.
- This drill is excellent for early season conditioning and can also be conducted indoors during inclement weather.

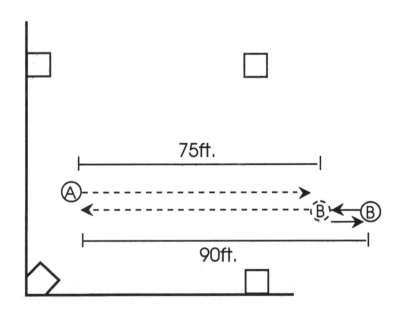

57 OVER-THE-SHOULDER CATCH

Objective: To practice catching a fly ball over the shoulder.

Equipment Needed: Gloves and baseballs.

Description: Every player is given a ball and is assigned to a line. Each line has a tosser, who begins the drill by standing to the left of the line. The first player (A) in line hands his baseball to the tosser and then sprints straight out under control. The tosser then throws a fly ball over player A's head so A must reach to catch the ball over his left shoulder. After catching or retrieving the ball, player A jogs back to the end of the line. The next player in line hands his ball to the tosser, and the drill continues.

Coaching Points:

- Variety can be added to the drill by having the tosser stand to the right of the line and throw the ball over the players' right shoulders.
- The key is to develop the ability to properly judge the path and speed of the thrown ball.

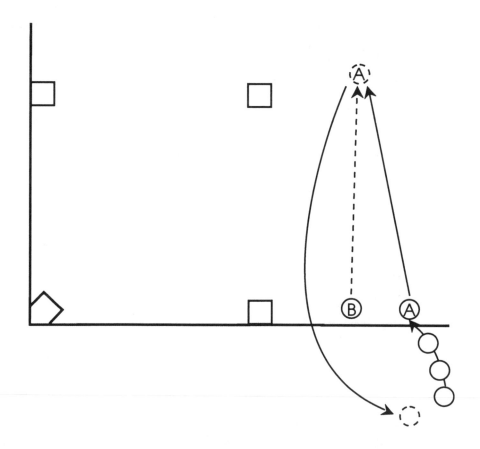

58 GOTCHA

Objective: To practice fielding balls hit directly at a player. To practice making accurate throws. To provide an inclement weather activity.

Equipment Needed: Gloves and tennis balls.

Description: The outfielders divide into two groups of three to four players each. If a team has more than eight outfielders, the number of groups or the size of each group can be increased. Remaining several feet apart, the two groups line up facing the gymnasium wall approximately 30 feet from the wall. A strip of tape should be placed at eye level on the wall to serve as a target. One player from each group participates in the drill at a time. The drill begins by having the first player in line one (A) throw a tennis ball at the tape on the wall. The first player in the other line (B) then plays the ball thrown off the wall. Both players receive points for accuracy and proficiency. Player A gets two points for a throw which hits the tape, one point for a throw within six inches of the tape, zero points for throws landing further than six inches from the tape, and minus one point for throws which do not come directly back at the two groups after hitting the wall. Player B gets two points for catching the ball on the fly off the wall, one point for fielding a single-bounce ball, zero points for fielding balls which bounce more than once, and minus one point for making an error or failing to field a ball judged as catchable. After the play, each player goes to the end of the other group's line. The drill continues as before. The first player to score a preset number of points wins.

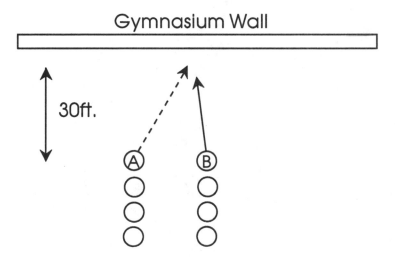

59   SPIN AND WIN

Objective: To practice fielding balls hit directly at a player. To practice making accurate throws. To develop the ability to pick up the location of the ball quickly. To provide for an inclement weather activity.

Equipment Needed: Gloves and tennis balls.

Description: The procedures for conducting this drill are the same as for the preceding drill, GOTCHA. This drill, however, requires that player B, who must field the tennis ball thrown off the wall, turns his back to the wall while player A is making his throw. Once the throw has been made, player A shouts, "Go." Player B then turns quickly, locates the ball, and fields the rebound.

Coaching Points:

- Variety can be added to the drill by eliminating the points that player A can earn and having A vary the type of throw he makes according to the type of rebound the coach wants. For example, a ball thrown hard against the floor first will result in a relatively high, lofty fly ball. A ball thrown easily against the floor will produce a relatively soft bouncer or fly ball.
- This drill emphasizes the need for players to stay alert and move quickly in any direction.

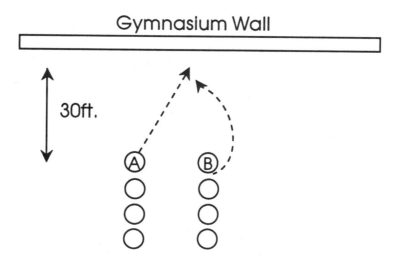

60 PIN POINT THROWS

Objective: To practice making accurate throws. To practice fielding and provide for and inclement weather activity.

Equipment Needed: Gloves and tennis balls.

Description: The drill involves having the outfielders forming a single line approximately 100 feet from and facing the gymnasium wall. A target area is taped on the wall. The target should be located approximately two feet from the gymnasium floor and be three feet long by two feet high. The coach stands in front of the target and serves as the judge of all throws. The first player in line (A) stands 40 feet in front of the coach and serves as the cutoff man. The next player in line (B) must field the tennis ball tossed to him. The drill begins by having player A toss a ground ball or a fly ball to B. Player B then fields the ball and throws it on a line at the target to A. Player A lines up between the coach and B. Player B concentrates on throwing the ball shoulder high and to the glove side of A. Player B attempts to make a throw which bounces only once before hitting the target. If the throw is off-line, the coach yells, "Cut, " and player A catches the throw. If the coach remains silent, the throw is allowed to go through to the wall. Points are awarded for the accuracy of player B's throw: two points for hitting the target squarely, one point for hitting the border of the target, and zero points for off-target throws. After two throws, the players rotate: player A goes to the end of the line, and player B becomes the cutoff man. The first player to earn a preset number of points wins.

Coaching Points:

- A shoulder-high, glove-side throw to the cutoff man makes it easier to handle the throw.
- Power can be added to the throw by using an overhand motion with a complete follow through while throwing.

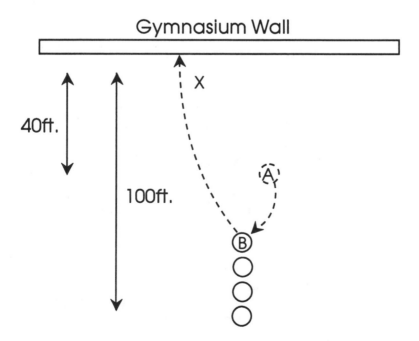

Gymnasium Wall

40ft.

100ft.

X

A

B

3

DEFENSIVE DRILLS

Catchers

61 GIVING SIGNS

Objective: To ensure that the catchers and the entire pitching staff fully understand the signs that the catchers will be using during a game.

Equipment Needed: Full catching gear for all catchers (optional).

Description: The drill involves all of the catchers and the pitchers on the team. The pitchers are spread out across the pitching mound area, reading the signs given by the catcher. The catchers form a line. The first catcher in line assumes his catching position behind home plate and gives a varying series of ten signs: pitches, pick offs, first and third signs, and pitch locations. The pitchers collectively read the signs, ensure that they were given clearly, and reach an agreement regarding their universal meaning. After giving the signs, the catcher moves to the end of the line. The next catcher in line takes his place, and the drill continues.

Coaching Points:

- This drill is particularly valuable when conducted before the season begins.
- This drill can be performed either indoors or outdoors.

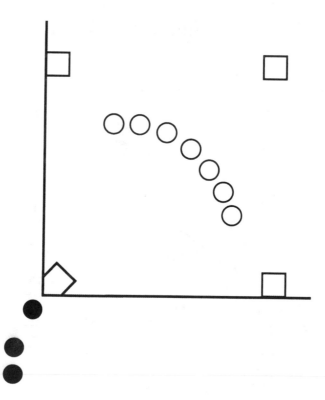

62 GIVING COMMANDS

Objective: To ensure that the catcher is cognizant of his many responsibilities behind home plate during the game. To practice using the proper verbal commands attendant to specific situations.

Equipment Needed: Full catching gear and gloves.

Description: The drill involves the entire infield. The drill begins by having the coach give the "game situation." The catcher then calls out the commands concerning the situation at hand. For example, in a bunt situation, the catcher calls out bunt defenses; on ground balls hit to the right side, he calls out, "get over there" to remind the pitcher to cover first base; when a baserunner is on third base, he sets the infield depths; on plays to the outfield, he lines up the relay men and calls out the relay commands; and during the course of the game, he is often asked to place the outfielders in their proper positions.

Coaching Points:

- This drill can be performed either indoors or outdoors.
- The catcher should be reminded that he has a leadership role during the game. He must get his defense in the right place at the right time.

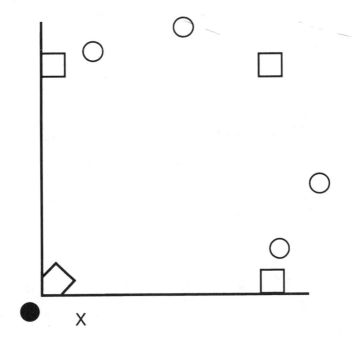

63 CATCH LIKE A CATCHER

Objective: To teach catchers to act, throw, and receive like catchers the moment they step onto the field.

Equipment Needed: Two catchers in full catcher's gear and a baseball.

Description: The   players play catch with each other, starting 60 feet apart and working back to 100 feet. They should catch the ball in a semi-crouched position (athletic position), getting their bodies and gloves behind each throw. They should use a short-arm throw to return the ball to their partner. This method of playing catch is designed to greatly improve the skills and techniques involved in both catching and throwing.

Coaching Points:

- Catchers should focus on quickly transferring the ball from their glove hand to their throwing hand, while they are torquing their upper bodies to throw (load position).
- Catchers should employ the quick, short-arm method of throwing.
- Like pitchers, catchers also "load and explode" while throwing.
- Like pitchers, catchers should keep their glove hands tucked when they throw to second base to get runners trying to steal. When catchers are having trouble throwing accurately, it is usually because of lead arm or glove hand problems.
- The Gillespie Hitting and Pitching Vest should be worn by catchers when engaged in drills which involve throwing to remind them to keep their front sides closed. This step should constantly reemphasize to the players to play "catch like a catcher."

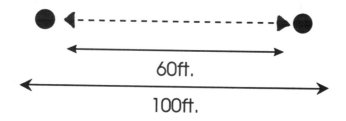

60ft.

100ft.

64 SELF CATCH AND BALL TRANSFER

Objective: To improve the ability to quickly get the ball to the "load or trigger" position. To develop the kinesthetic sense for turning the ball to grip it across the seams. To practice the techniques involved in assuming the proper position for throwing.

Equipment Needed: One baseball glove per player.

Description: The drill involves having a player repeatedly fire the ball into his glove, bring the ball out of the glove, and move into a throwing position as quickly as possible. This is a very important drill to get the "feel" of a baseball and practice the mechanics of getting into the proper position for throwing as quickly as possible.

65 PHANTOM BALL

Objective: To warm up prior to actually throwing a baseball. To practice the proper movement mechanics involved in throwing.

Equipment Needed: Full catching gear including gloves.

Description: Wearing his full catching gear, a player should simulate throwing a baseball without throwing it. The focus should be on playing "catch like a catcher" and then raising up and throwing a "phantom" ball with an emphasis on proper wrist action and full arm movement.

Coaching Points:

- Catchers should "explode" their throwing arms and "pop" their wrists.
- Figuratively speaking, you should be able to hear their hands cutting through the air.
- The fact that hand and wrist action are extremely important in gaining throwing velocity should be emphasized.

66 UNDERLOAD THROWING

Objective: To practice the proper mechanics and techniques of throwing in a manner which places less strain on the arm.

Equipment Needed: Gloves, catcher's equipment, several two or three ounce underloaded balls, and a net.

Description: From 30 feet, the throwing catcher fires an underloaded ball at a target which has been taped or marked on a net. Another catcher retrieves the ball at the foot of the net and throws it back to the first catcher, who upon catching the ball fires the ball back at the target on the net. After fifteen throws, the players exchange positions. The drill should be continued for a preset number of throws.

Coaching Points:

- This drill would be beneficial for all players.
- Variety can be added to this drill by varying either the distance the ball must be thrown or the location of the target on the net.

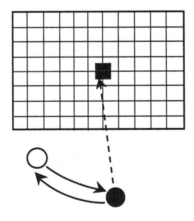

67 SHIFT DRILL - NO HANDS

Objective: To help catchers learn to shift on pitches in the dirt and to block the ball with their bodies while keeping their hands behind their backs, sliding right or left, and never letting the ball get past them. To develop lateral quickness by working the abductor and adductor thigh muscles.

Equipment Needed: Full catching equipment, several baseballs, and a home plate.

Description: The drill involves players working in pairs: one as a receiver and one as a thrower. The receiving catcher gets behind the plate in a receiving stance, tucks his hands behind his back, blocks balls thrown into the dirt to his right and left, and attempts to funnel blocked balls back toward home plate. The thrower throws fairly hard one-hoppers from a distance of approximately 25 feet from the plate. After 15 throws, the players exchange positions. The drill continues for a preset number of blocked throws.

Coaching Points:

- The key is to have the receiving catcher get squarely behind the ball with his body angled toward home plate in order to funnel all balls back to the plate.
- The catchers should be taught to react first with their bodies and not their hands. They should cushion the ball and catch it with their bodies. Once they conceive of this idea, blocking will become easier and surer.
- Catchers can also perform this drill alone, without equipment, by imagining a pitch coming at them in the dirt and blocking the imaginary ball.
- The drill can be performed progressively by having the throwing catcher initially call out the location of his throws and subsequently require the receiver to be ready to go any direction.

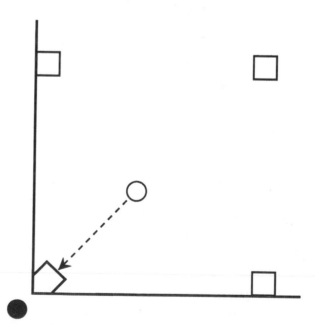

68 SHIFT DRILL - WITH HANDS

Objective: To help catchers learn how to use their bodies and their hands to block throws and pitches. To practice proper footwork for shifting. To develop lateral quickness by working the abductor and the adductor muscles.

Equipment Needed: Full catching gear, baseballs, and a home plate.

Description: The procedures for conducting this drill are exactly the same as for the preceding drill, with the exception of the fact that in this drill catchers should use their gloves and bodies to block the ball. Their hands should be used to protect their groin area and block the opening that might otherwise exist in the groin area. They should not try to catch the ball with their hands. Their chin should be in a tucked position (pressed downward towards their throat) to protect their Adam's apple. After a preset number of repetitions, the players rotate positions.

Coaching Points:

- Catchers should attempt to catch the ball with their belly button and chest and knock it back toward home plate.
- This drill should be mastered to the point that it is instinctive.

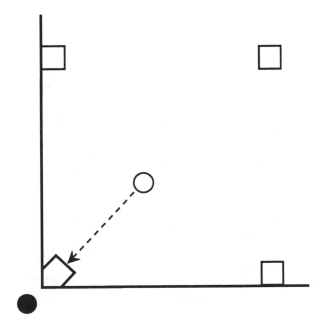

69 BLOCK AND SCRAMBLE

Objective: To practice blocking a wild pitch in the dirt, scrambling after the ball, and throwing a baserunner out at second base.

Equipment Needed: Full catching gear, baseballs, and gloves.

Description: The procedures for conducting this drill are the same as for the preceding drill, "Shift Drill: With Hands," with a few exceptions. In this drill, the catcher must scramble for the ball after he blocks it and quickly throw it to second base. An extra player is needed to catch the throws to second base (A). Depending on the number of players available, another player could be incorporated into the drill to serve as a baserunner attempting to take second base on the blocked ball. After a preset number of plays, the players switch positions.

Coaching Points:

- If extra players are available, variety could be added to the drill by incorporating another baserunner (this one at second base) and two more infielders: a first baseman and a third baseman. The catcher could then throw to any base (to catch runners off base or to catch a runner stealing third).
- The drill should be conducted with minimal rest: the players should be kept working at all times.

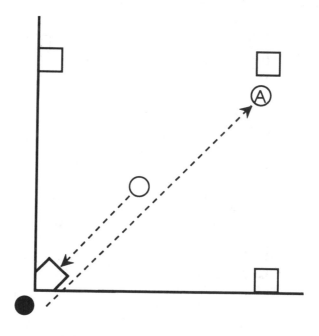

70 GOALIE

Objective: To practice blocking skills. To improve reaction time. To foster competition.

Equipment Needed: Full catching gear, baseballs, and two goals (hockey nets).

Description: Two goals are set up approximately five feet apart. The catcher assumes a ready (catching) position between the goals. Another player (or the coach) stands facing the catcher 40 to 50 feet directly in front of the goals. The objective of the game is to have the player in front of the catcher attempt to throw a ball, which must hit the dirt in front of the net to count, into the nets. The catcher attempts to keep the throw from the nets. One point is earned for either each successful block or each throw into the net. Either a preset number of plays or a preset number of earned points constitutes a game.

Coaching Points:

- Variety can be added to the drill by having the catcher scramble after each blocked ball.
- The player attempting to throw the ball into the net should vary his throws (location and intensity).

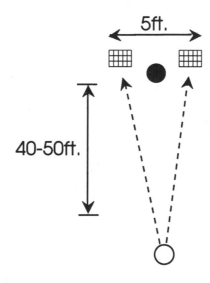

71 ON THE BUTTON

Objective: To practice making quick, accurate throws to each base.

Equipment Needed: Full catching gear, baseballs, and gloves.

Description: The drill involves three players: a catcher (A), and a player (B), usually another catcher, who serves as the infielder who covers the base, and a player (C) who acts as the pitcher. In some instances, a coach may decide to act as the pitcher. The drill is initiated by having player C, who is standing approximately 25 feet in front of A, throw (pitch) the ball to A. From a ready position stand, player A receives the "pitch" and fires it to B at first base. After 10 throws to first base, player B moves to the next base. Player A then throws 10 times to second base. The same scenario is then repeated at third base. Before the three players switch positions, the entire sequence is repeated, five throws to each of the three bases, for a total of 45 throws by player A.

Coaching Points:

- The drill can be performed without a pitcher (C). Player A simply feigns receiving a pitch and then fires to B who is standing 90 feet away.
- Using proper throwing mechanics should be emphasized at all times.

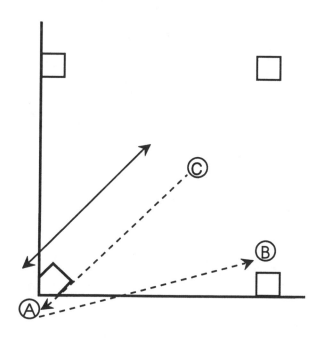

72 TAG PLAY AT HOME

Objective: To practice blocking the plate and applying the tag on a sliding runner. To develop the ability to bounce up after a tag play and throw to second base to get a batter attempting to advance to second base on the throw to the plate.

Equipment Needed: Full catching gear and baseballs.

Description: The drill initially involves two catchers: one at "home plate" (A) and one approximately 100 feet away (B). The drill begins by having player B throw to the "plate" to A. Player A assumes a position with his left shin guard about a foot in front of home plate in order to block the plate. Player A, however, leaves the outside of the plate "unprotected" for the baserunner to aim at with his slide. As he receives the throw, player A quickly gets into a kneeling position with his right knee. Player A holds the ball in his bare hand which he covers with his glove to protect them from the baserunner's spikes. As he catches the ball, player A makes a swipe tag on the imaginary baserunner on the outside of the plate that was offered to the runner. Player A gets the tag "in and out" as fast as possible. Player A then springs up and fires the ball to B who then goes through the same sequence of actions. The drill continues for a preset number of plays.

Coaching Points:

- The drill can be expanded by adding an actual baserunner. In this instance, a coach may want to make the drill more "injury-proof." For example, the drill may be conducted on a grassy area. The baserunner should not wear spikes. The catcher must keep his mask on to help protect himself during the resulting collision with the baserunner.
- Adhering to the proper mechanics for throwing should be emphasized.

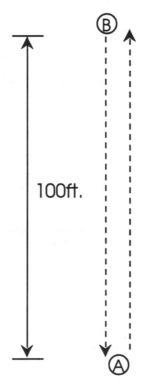

100ft.

73 STOPWATCH

Objective: To practice making quick, accurate throws to second base. To make catchers more aware of the need to throw quickly.

Equipment Needed: Baseballs, gloves, and a stopwatch.

Description: The drill involves a catcher (A), a pitcher (B), another catcher (C) who serves as the infielder, and a coach. The drill begins by having player B (who is on the mound) throw to A. Player A receives the pitch and throws as quickly and as accurately as possible to C in an attempt to throw out an imaginary baserunner. Player C takes the throw, makes a swipe tag, and tosses the ball back to B. The drill continues for a set number of plays. Using a stopwatch, the coach times player A's throws to second base. From the moment the pitch initially touches player A's glove to when C receives A's throw, the elapsed time should not exceed two seconds.

Coaching Points:

- Throws to first base and third base should also be practiced and timed.
- A "good" time for throwing to a base is 1.6 seconds.

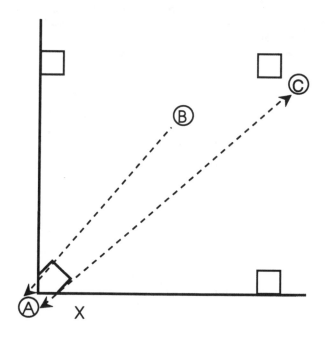

74 PASSED BALL

Objective: To teach catchers to scramble after a passed ball, retrieve it, and make a snap throw from a kneeling position to the pitcher covering home plate.

Equipment Needed: Full catching gear, baseballs, and a home plate.

Description: The drill involves two catchers, both in full gear. One player (A) assumes a catcher's stance in the catcher's box. The other player (B) stands next to home plate. The drill begins by having player A flip the ball behind himself about 20 feet. Player A then races after the ball, slides on his knees alongside the ball, scoops the ball into his throwing hand, and makes a knee high, snap throw to B who is "covering" home plate. After a preset number of plays, the players switch roles.

Coaching Points:

- Catchers retrieving passed balls should always approach the ball with their glove hand side ready to open up to home plate.
- The key to making a "good" scoop (pick-up) of the ball is for the catcher to get alongside the ball in his slide and to use his glove hand to simultaneously scoop the ball into his (bare) throwing hand.

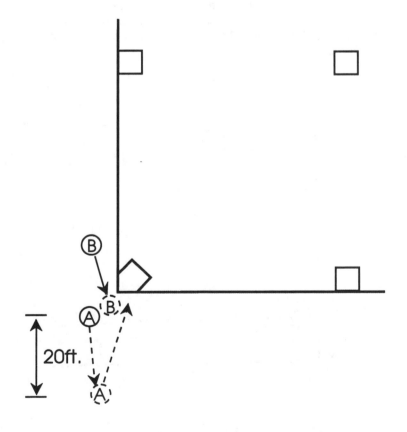

75 POP-UPS

Objective: To practice the techniques and footwork involved in catching pop flies.

Equipment Needed: Full catching gear, baseballs, home plate, and a fungo bat.

Description: The drill involves having a coach hit (or throw simulated) pop-ups around home plate to the catcher. The catcher practices the techniques and fundamentals involved in fielding pop-ups. The catcher's initial step is to remove his mask and locate the ball. He then throws his mask far enough away so that he won't trip over it. If the ball is hit directly above home plate, the catcher turns his back toward the infield, because a pop-up off the bat has backspin which will cause it to drift toward the pitcher's mound. The catcher should stay behind the ball and always catch it chest-to-head high, if possible. His hands should be extended about 18 inches from his chest. He should always catch the ball out in front of his body. Using a single-break glove is preferred because it enables the catcher to get his thumb parallel to the ground and underneath the ball.

Coaching Points:

- This drill can be conducted either outdoors or indoors. Outdoors in the sun is preferred. If performed indoors, the drill should involve tossing the ball in the direction of a gymnasium light. The catcher can use either his glove or his bare hand to screen the sun or the gym light while lining up the ball.
- The drill can be expanded to include other players. The coach can hit or throw pop-ups to several players at a time. Players can also hit or throw pop-ups to each other.

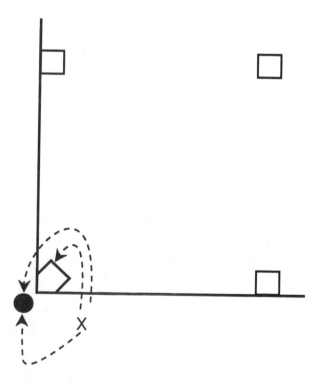

76 FRAMING THE STRIKE ZONE

Objective: To teach catchers to frame and keep borderline pitches in the strike zone.

Equipment Needed: Full catching gear, baseballs, and a home plate.

Description: The drill involves two players: a catcher (A) and his partner (B), preferably another catcher. The drill is initiated by having player A assume his receiver's stance. Standing 25 feet in front of and facing player A, B points at various locations on the perimeter of the strike zone. Player A extends his glove and catches each "phantom" pitch. The coach watches the action to ensure that player A is working his glove properly and holding pitches in the strike zone. He makes corrections and offers suggestions to player A as needed. Once the basic techniques have been mastered, the drill is expanded to actual throwing. Player A and B throw balls to each other and concentrate on using the proper mechanics and techniques for receiving each throw.

Coaching Points:

- This drill is particularly beneficial in the early weeks of the season.
- The drill should focus on enabling catchers to develop soft hands and the ability to properly frame pitches. Being able to properly frame pitches can make a difference in as much as 25% of the pitches thrown in a game in keeping balls in the strike zone.

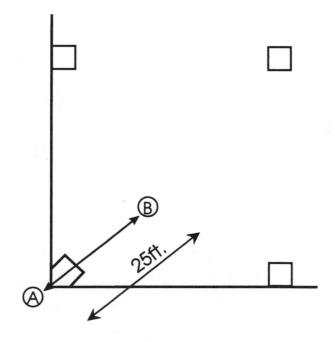

77 DUGOUT GOALIE

Objective: To practice keeping overthrown balls from going into the dugout area. To emphasize the importance of preventing the ball from leaving the playing area.

Equipment Needed: Full catching gear, baseballs, gloves, and two red cones.

Description: The drill involves two catchers: a player (A) is serving as the catcher and a player (B) who tosses the ball to A to retrieve. A hypothetical tactical situation is established where a ground ball has been hit with no runners on base. Two red cones are placed five to ten feet apart, approximately 40 feet from player A, to designate the "dugout area." The drill begins by having player B yell "Now" and then roll the ball to the dugout (the red cones). On the call, player A breaks on a 45-degree angle for the dugout in an attempt to keep the ball from "getting into" the dugout. By protecting the dugout, A helps prevent a baserunner from advancing to second base. After a preset number of plays, the players switch roles.

Coaching Points:

- If necessary, the distance that player A has to run to the dugout can be shortened.
- The drill can be expanded by having player A scramble to his feet after retrieving the ball thrown by B and throw a strike toward second base (to player B).

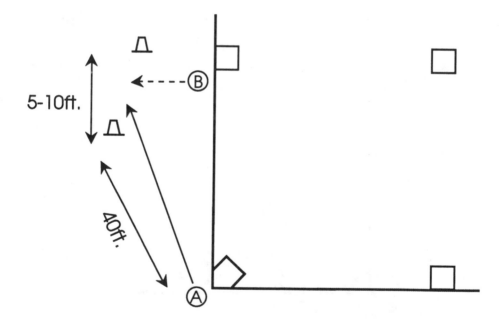

78 FORCE PLAY– DOUBLE PLAY

Objective: To enable catchers to practice making the plate tag on a force-out at home, then stepping quickly toward the pitcher's mound, and throwing to first base.

Equipment Needed: Full catching gear, baseballs, gloves, a home plate, and a first base.

Description: The drill involves three players: two catchers and a first baseman. One catcher (A) serves as the home plate catcher, while the other catcher (B) lines up in the infield, 30 feet in front of A. The first baseman (C) assumes a position on the first base bag, 90 feet from home plate. Player B initiates the drill by throwing the ball to A (who has given him a glove target). Player A places his right foot on the infield edge of home plate and his left foot in front of the plate in a comfortable position. Player A assumes a semi-crouch position awaiting for what he hopes will be a chest-high force-play throw. As soon as he receives the throw, player A pushes off the plate. Using a crow-hop step, he fires the ball to the inside of the first base bag to C. Player A makes 10 plays and then switches positions with B.

Coaching Points:

- If player B's throw to home is wild, A must adjust as needed, tag the plate as best he can, and decide whether he can complete the double play. If he thinks he can't, he shouldn't risk a wild throw.
- If player A is off balance after tagging home, he generally should not throw to first base.

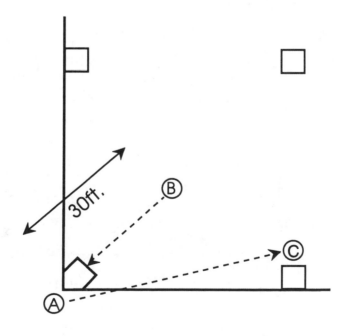

4

DEFENSIVE DRILLS

Pitching

79   SAND CAN EXERCISE

Objective: To stretch and strengthen a pitcher's throwing arm. To serve as part of the daily warm-up routine.

Equipment Needed: One sand can per player. (A sand can is a tennis ball can, filled with approximately three pounds of sand, which has been taped at both ends.)

Description: Each player performs each of the exercises illustrated below on a daily basis. Each exercise is done at a relatively slow pace in order to safely force the muscles and ligaments of the throwing arm to perform the desired work/movement. Approximately 10 repetitions of each exercise should be performed.

Coaching Points:

- Sand can exercises should be performed on a daily basis by all team members, not just the pitchers.
- If necessary, the amount of sand in the can may be either increased or decreased as needed. As a result, each player should tape his name on his sand can.

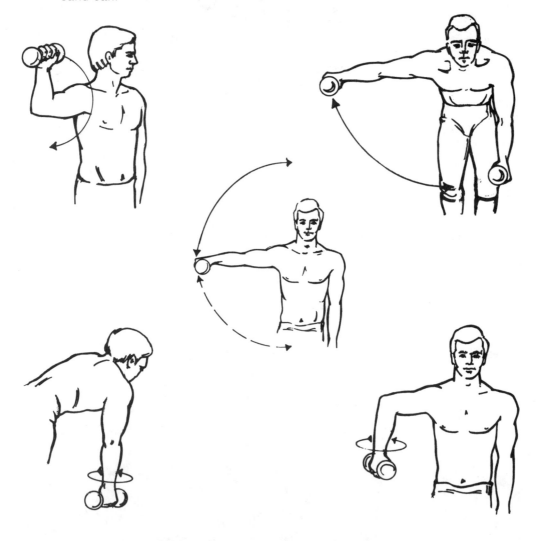

80 TUBING EXERCISES

Objective: To stretch and strengthen the throwing muscles; to serve as part of the daily warm-up routine.

Equipment Needed: One 20-inch long piece of basic surgical (rubber) tubing per player.

Description: Each pitcher performs each of the exercises illustrated below on a daily basis. The exercises can either be performed with a partner or individually. As a general rule, these exercises are done by pairs of players early in the season. One player holds the tubing, while the other performs the specific exercise movement by pulling on the tubing. Each exercise is done at a relatively slow pace in order to safely force the muscles and ligaments of the throwing arm to perform the desired work/movement. Approximately 10 repetitions of each exercise should be performed. Later in the season, a player can do the exercises by himself, simply by anchoring the tubing to a fixed object, such as a door, while doing the exercises.

Coaching Points:

- Tubing exercises should be performed on a daily basis by all team members, not just the pitchers.
- A personalized routine of tubing exercises can be developed to meet the unique or specific needs of a player.

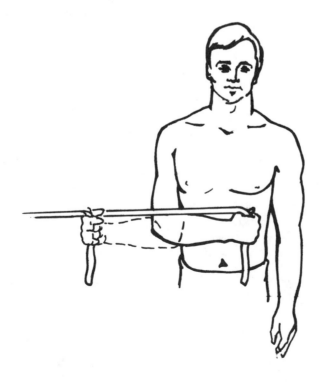

81 PHANTOM PITCHING

Objective: To stretch the body by having the pitcher perform a series of pitching-related movements after doing a bend-over stretching exercise. To warm up the body without undue strain on the throwing arm.

Equipment Needed: One pitching vest and glove per player.

Description: The drill involves pitchers working in a group. One player acts as the exercise leader for the group and calls out commands to the group. Each player has his glove on and wears a securely fastened pitching vest to aid in glove-arm action. The first command is "From the windup, number one." Without a baseball, all of the pitchers then wind up and throw a simulated pitch. (Note: No strain is placed on the pitching arm because the pitchers are not using a baseball.) Each pitcher is required to use good mechanics: strong wrist action and a complete follow-through motion which is designed to specifically stretch the muscles of the back. Twenty-five repetitions of the bend over, simulated pitches are performed from both the windup and the stretch. The group leader calls out the situation and the specific repetition each time, "from the windup, number two." Players also are required to perform 10 simulated pick-off throws to first base.

Coaching Points:

- Going through the pitching motion helps to reinforce "muscle memory" and "proper mechanics."
- Once the pitching mechanics have been mastered, the drill can be varied by having the coach call out bunt situations during the from-the-stretch repetitions to which the pitcher must react: field an imaginary bunt, turn, and simulate throwing to a specific base.

82 SELF-CATCH

Objective: To gain the "feel" of the baseball, and to develop wrist pop.

Equipment Needed: Baseballs and gloves.

Description: Players work individually. Each pitcher "pops" the ball from his throwing hand into his glove hand. The pitcher uses a variety of grips while performing the drill: curve ball, split finger, change ups, cross seam fastball. The wrist snap should be emphasized. The pitchers should attempt to gain a "touch" and "feel" for the baseball. They should experiment with different grips, particularly with the seams.

Coaching Points:

- Many successful coaches and pitchers believe that "wrist explosion or popping" is the most important factor in the mechanics of pitching.
- A pitcher should be encouraged while performing the drill to mentally "pitch a game." He should imagine various situations and react accordingly, for example, two strikes on the batter, baserunners on first and third.

83 JOHNNY SAIN'S SPIN DRILL

Objective: To teach pitchers how to throw the breaking ball. To develop an understanding of the rotation of the ball.

Equipment Needed: A Johnny Sain Pitching Device (A baseball on a long spike that runs through the ball. The ball rotates on the spike like a world globe).

Description: The drill involves having the pitcher grip the ball and work on the spin and wrist rotation for a curve ball. The drill should last 5 to 10 minutes per player.

Coaching Points:

- This is an extremely effective drill for getting the "feel" of the curve ball and actually seeing the spin of the ball.

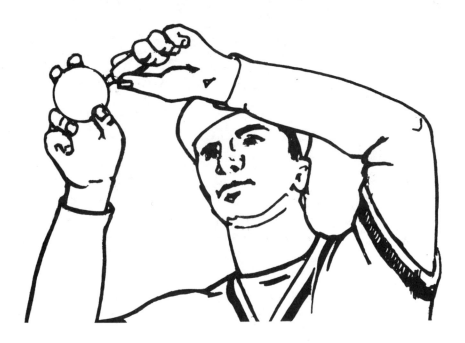

84 CHAIN DRILL

Objective: To emphasize the back-bend and the follow-through aspects of proper pitching mechanics. To promote throwing over the stride leg and rolling the back foot.

Equipment Needed: Baseballs, gloves, a pitching vest, and a folding chair.

Description: The drill involves two players: a pitcher and a receiver. The pitcher places his throwing (pivot) foot on the seat of a chair (right foot: right-handed pitcher, left foot: left-handed pitcher), with the foot flat on its side with the ankle turned in and pointed towards the catcher. The stride foot should be planted on the ground in front of the chair in a landing position (toe turned in: a closed position). The drill involves having the pitcher practice throwing from this position to his partner who is approximately 30 feet away in a receiver's crouch giving him a glove target. The pitcher throws easy curve balls, while concentrating on pulling his upper body over the thigh of his landing foot.

Coaching Points:

- Particular emphasis should be put on following through when throwing the curve ball.
- The drill could also involve having the pitcher throw at a target taped onto a net.
- This drill reinforces the baseball expression that throwing a curve requires a pitcher to ''pull the body over'' or ''pull that curve ball down.''
- This drill should not involve throwing hard. The pitcher should be required to perform a relatively high number of repetitions.

85   BAT DRILL

Objective: To practice the proper mechanical sequence of opening the hips and throwing over the stride leg.

Equipment Needed: A bat or broomstick.

Description: The pitcher places the bat behind his back, and holds it in place with his elbows. This action freezes and isolates the pitcher's upper body, enabling him to fully concentrate on properly opening his hips. Starting in a gathered (top of his windup) position, the pitcher then strides toward the plate as if he were pitching. He concentrates on pointing the end of the bat he's holding at the plate for as long as possible before throwing. Then, as the bat turns, his hips have opened. His hips should not open until they reach a point as close to the plate as possible in order to generate maximum power.

Coaching Points: When the knee of the pitcher's stride leg begins to rotate toward the plate, his hips will start to open at the same time.

86 WINDING DRILL

Objective: To promote balance; to practice the gathered position. To practice the technique of slightly pausing at the top of the pitcher's windup.

Equipment Needed: Pitcher's mound and baseballs.

Description: The drill involves having the pitcher start his windup without a baseball. When he's in the gathered position, the coach (or another pitcher) places a baseball in his throwing hand. As soon as he gets the ball, the pitcher resumes his delivery motion. Initially, the pitcher completes his delivery but does not throw the ball. The drill can subsequently be expanded to have the pitcher actually throw to a receiver.

Coaching Points:

- In order to develop proper balance in his pitcher, the coach can wait any length of time before giving up the baseball.
- During the drill, the coach should stand to the side of the pitcher, toward either first base (for left-handers) or third base (for right-handers).

87 BRICK DRILL

Objective: To practice proper back leg action while pitching. To help prevent foot drag and overstriding in the pitcher's delivery.

Equipment Needed: A regular (red) brick or brick-sized piece of two by four inch wood.

Description: The pitcher assumes the stretch position. He places the brick a few inches in front of his pivot foot. The drill involves having the pitcher throw using normal delivery. If his back foot hits the brick, either his foot is dragging or he's overstriding. The ongoing purpose of this drill is to remind the pitcher to roll and lift his back foot.

Coaching Points:

- A six inch drag with the toe of the back foot is permissible. A two foot trail in the dirt indicates a clear need to work on this drill.

88 PROPER LEG SWING ACTION

Objective: To practice the correct stride-leg action when getting into the gathered (top of the windup) position.

Equipment Needed: None.

Description: The pitcher starts in the stretch position, except that he places his stride foot on the second-base side of his pivot foot. With his stride foot above the rubber, he then lifts his leg straight up to the gathered position, pauses, and completes his delivery. By adjusting his foot in this manner, he makes it virtually impossible to swing his leg.

Coaching Points:

- Some pitchers prefer to swing their stride leg up and back behind them during the pitching motion as opposed to the correct approach of just lifting their stride leg and slightly rotating their hips.
- Leg swinging can cause a pitcher to unduly rush the movement mechanics of his lower body.
- Pitchers who have a serious problem with their stride-leg action mechanics should be encouraged (or required) to perform this on a regular basis until proper stride-leg action becomes a habit.

89 PROPER FOOT-UNDER-KNEE ACTION

Objective: To practice keeping the foot under the knee during the delivery.

Equipment Needed: A folding chair.

Description: The drill involves placing the back of a chair in the path of the pitcher to provide a means of determining whether his lead foot strays too far during his delivery. The pitcher must pitch the ball without kicking the chair. When he is able to throw the ball without his lead foot hitting the chair, his lead foot is in the proper position (very likely under his knee).

Coaching Points:

- Many pitchers prefer to have their foot out away from their body. Such a body position, however, may cause the pitcher to lean backward to compensate.
- Because not keeping his lead foot under his knee during the delivery is a relatively hard habit to break, a pitcher should spend as much time as needed performing this drill.

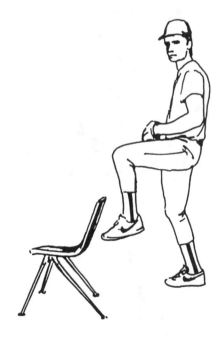

90 PROPER FINGER POSITION

Objective: To encourage the proper position of the fingers while griping the ball in the "T" position.

Equipment Needed: Baseballs.

Description: The pitcher kneels on his pivot-leg knee with his stride foot aimed at the plate. The drill involves having the pitcher put his throwing arm in the "T" position with his fingers on top of the ball. In order to get a better feel of his fingers being on top of the ball, he then watches his ball hand during the throwing motion. His fingers go from being on top to being behind the ball during his throwing motion.

Coaching Points:

- Ideally, the pitcher would throw the ball into a net to complete his delivery during this drill.
- Once the pitcher has developed a "feel" for the ball in the "T" position, he should perform the drill by practicing breaking his hands in a thumbs-down fashion and watch his hands "break."

91 PROPER ARM SWING ACTION

Objective: To practice the mechanics of the proper arm swing behind the pitcher's body.

Equipment Needed: Baseballs.

Description: The pitcher kneels on his pivot-leg knee with his stride foot aimed at the plate (target) and his hands together. The drill begins by having the pitcher break his hands. He then watches his arm swing as it goes down, back, and up to the fully extended "T" position. The pitcher should concentrate on keeping his shoulders lined up to the target so no rotation can occur. As a result, his arm is prevented from going behind his body during his pitching motion.

Coaching Points:

- Many pitchers have wasted movement in their deliveries by going back and behind their bodies during the throwing motion. After the break, the pitcher's arm movement should only be down and back (not behind).
- Excessively moving the arm behind his body may result in too much upper body rotation and unwanted arm drag.
- In most instances, the typical reason pitchers swing their arms behind their bodies is they put their hands in the improper position at the top of the windup. The farther away a pitcher's hands are from his body, the more likely he will move his arm behind his body while he is pitching.

92 PROPER FRONT-SHOULDER ACTION

Objective: To practice the mechanics of properly moving the front shoulder during the delivery.

Equipment Needed: Baseballs.

Description: The pitcher kneels on his pivot-leg knee with his stride foot aimed at the plate (target). He starts from the "T" position with his front elbow aiming at the target. The drill involves having the pitcher use his elbow as a reference sight to the target. He then initiates his throwing motion by tucking his glove into his side and bringing his throwing shoulder forward toward the target. Throughout the drill, he observes the front side of his body to get a "feel" for what constitutes proper front shoulder movement.

Coaching Points:

- Many pitchers, particularly those who throw hard, prefer to aim their front shoulders up over the batter's head while throwing. A pitcher's front shoulder, however, should be aimed at the target until it has rolled under the pitcher's torso as a result of the acceleration of the ball.
- When the pitcher's shoulder rolls under, his glove should be tucked into his side.
- When the pitcher has mastered the techniques involved in this drill, the drill can be varied by having the pitcher start the drill from the break point (as opposed to a "T" position).

93 PROPER FOLLOW-THROUGH ACTION

Objective: To practice full extension and follow-through with the throwing arm; to discourage recoiling the arm after releasing the ball.

Equipment Needed: Baseballs.

Description: The pitcher kneels on his pivot-leg knee with his stride foot aimed at the plate (target). The drill involves having a pitcher throw the ball at less-than-full speed. After releasing the ball, the pitcher tries to touch the numbers on the back of his jersey in one smooth extension of his arm which moves through the natural route of his follow through.

Coaching Points:

- The pitcher can throw the ball either into a net or to a receiver.
- Recoiling the arm after releasing the pitch (which many pitchers unfortunately like to do) can lead to a serious injury to the throwing arm.
- This drill should not be performed at full speed under any conditions.

94 STAYING BEHIND THE BALL

Objective: To have a pitcher practice keeping his hand behind the ball when releasing it while throwing it; to develop the ability not to "cut" the ball when throwing it.

Equipment Needed: A half-white and half-black baseball.

Description: This drill can be performed in a variety of body positions. The drill involves having a pitcher play catch with another player and use a specific type of grip when throwing the ball. The pitcher should grip the ball so that one finger is in the white area of the ball, one is in the black portion, and his thumb is on the border between the two colors. When playing catch, if the pitcher is gripping the ball properly, he will see two distinct halves of the ball while the ball is in flight, if he is staying behind the pitch. If not, he will see a flutter of black and white.

Coaching Points:

- Cutting the ball (throwing the ball slightly off center) will decrease the velocity of a pitch.
- This drill should be incorporated into a pitcher's daily workout regimen if he is having trouble staying behind the ball.

95 FIGURE-8

Objective: To develop pitching rhythm. To practice the proper pitching mechanics concerning trunk rotation, back swing, arm elevation, and the appropriate path of the throwing arm (up to down) in one continuous movement.

Equipment Needed: Any ball that holds air (a volleyball, soccer ball, or basketball) for each player.

Description: The pitcher stands sideways to an imaginary home plate in the stretch position with a ball held in both of his hands extended from his body. Simulating using the ball as a large piece of chalk on a blackboard, he makes a "figure-8" movement as if he were drawing an "8" lying on its side. His hands start down and backwards, then up and over his head, then forward and down, then up to complete the sideways "8" figure.

Coaching Points:

- It is recommended that four or five balls be kept in the equipment bag for pitchers to use daily.
- Doing this drill two or three minutes daily will greatly reinforce many of the critical factors involved in proper pitching mechanics.

96 "FLAMINGO:" THROWING FROM UP POSITION

Objective: To prevent the pitcher from rushing his delivery to home plate. Rushing the delivery is the number one nemesis of all pitchers, and the cause of most sore arms.

Equipment Needed: Baseballs, gloves, and pitching vests.

Description: The pitcher stands sideways to home plate in the stretch position and brings his throwing arm to its highest elevation. He has his glove hand tucked and his landing leg raised and cocked. On command from the coach, he delivers the ball to his pitching partner. The coach calls, "Load" (pause), "Explode" (throw), and "Follow through." From this "flamingo" position, a pitcher should be able to throw at approximately 75% of his normal pitching velocity.

Coaching Points:

- When the pitcher rushes his delivery, his body opens up too soon, forcing the path of his throwing arm to take a "shortcut," thereby preventing it from reaching the proper elevation point above his head.
- In taking a shortened course to catch up to his body, the pitcher's arm will pass his head about ear-high, causing him to be wild, up and in.
- When a pitcher rushes his pitches (which many coaches refer to as "throwing only with his arm"), more pressure and strain are placed on his arm because his body "leaves early."

97 OFFSET PITCHING

Objective: To aid pitchers who appear to be completely "out of sync" and struggling to find their control. To teach pitchers to make mechanical adjustments.

Equipment Needed: Ball and gloves.

Description: The catcher, instead of lining up behind home plate in his normal position, lines up "offset" to one side or the other in either batting box and makes the pitcher throw 10 throws to his left, then 10 to his right, and then 10 straight at him.

Coaching Points:

- When a pitcher is preparing to pitch, warming up in the bullpen or pitching in a game, he has to make physical corrections all the time to get the ball where he wants it. This drill exaggerates the need to be able to make necessary corrections.
- As a general rule, the particular location that usually requires the most attention is placing the catcher in the left-handed batter's box with a right-handed pitcher throwing.
- Most pitching problems come from rushing the delivery, which causes the pitcher to be wild inside, for example, when a right-handed pitcher is throwing into the right-handed batter's box. As a result, in this situation, to make the mechanical adjustment, the catcher should cross over to the left-handed batter's box and have the pitcher make the necessary adjustments to throw to the newly positioned target.

98 JAPANESE CATCH

Objective: To improve a pitcher's control by requiring him to throw strikes from a relatively long distance.

Equipment Needed: Baseballs and gloves.

Description: The pitcher warms up at 75 to 80 feet and reduces the distance gradually until he reaches the normal pitching distance of 60' 6". Obviously, the task of hitting the target (the catcher's glove) becomes easier as the pitcher gets closer to the target.

Coaching Points:

- It is recommended that a pitcher make only 20 to 25 throws before he gets to the normal pitching distance.
- Japanese pitchers use this training method to improve their control.

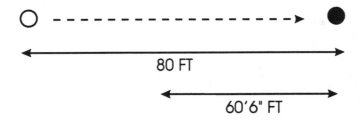

99 CROW-HOP CATCH

Objective: To have the pitcher practice throwing from his back foot, to help prevent him from rushing his body.

Equipment Needed: Baseballs and gloves.

Description: From 60 to 70 feet apart, two pitchers play glove-target catch, taking a short "crow hop" onto their back foot with every delivery of the baseball. The player receiving the throw should assume a catcher's crouch and give a glove target to the pitcher.

Coaching Points:

- Pitchers should be reminded of why they're doing this drill.
- Coaches should emphasize to pitchers to throw from their back foot and not to "rush" their bodies.
- In most instances, performing this drill for five to ten minutes is sufficient.

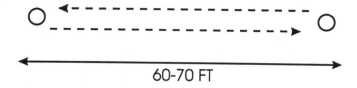

60-70 FT

100 UNDERLOAD

Objective: To practice the proper mechanics of the pitching motion as frequently as possible with minimal strain on the throwing arm.

Equipment Needed: Two two- or three-ounce underload balls at each station, a net to throw the ball into, and a home plate.

Description: Player A throws an underload ball into netting approximately 30 feet away. A strike zone should be taped onto the netting. His partner (B) stands close to the net to serve as a batter (to simulate a game situation). Player B keeps his glove on to protect himself against being hit by a pitch. Player A throws 15 pitches from both the windup and from a stretch position, using all of his pitches: curve, fastball, change-up, etc. The players trade positions after 15 pitches until each has thrown a total of 75 to 90 pitches. This drill can also be conducted on a competitive basis. For example, an entire underload ball or Whiffle ball game may be played with positional players hitting at a 30-foot distance, and the pitcher pitching as if in the last game of the World Series. Rules can be set up in such a way to encourage players to have fun. Pitchers can get an outstanding mechanical workout, using all pitches. The drill could also help hitters prepare for an actual game.

Coaching Points:

- Pitchers should be encouraged to throw underload balls as hard as they can; they should not be afraid of hurting their arms.
- One recommendation is to use this drill once every other day, using two-ounce balls for 10 days, then three-ounce balls for 10 days. A pitcher can throw the regular six-ounce baseball one day, then use underload balls the next day.
- Underload balls can be used to stretch out between starts during the regular season.

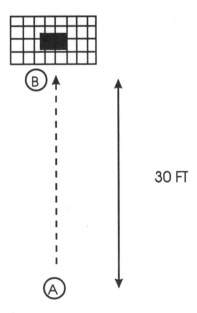

30 FT

101 WALL BALL– RUBBER BALL GAME

Objective: To practice pitching and work on control.

Equipment Needed: A rubber ball of regulation size and weight, chalk, a home plate, and a wall.

Description: A strike zone is drawn on a concrete wall in chalk. On each side of the strike zone, an outline of an imaginary batter is also drawn. The drill involves having a pitcher set up at the proper pitching distance (60' 6") from the wall. He then pitches an imaginary game against the wall, using all of his pitches and his imagination. He keeps the count, outs, innings, and score.

Coaching Points:

- The pitcher can throw as many innings as he chooses.
- The drill figuratively allows a pitcher to throw in a "competitive" game any day he wishes...and be a winner.
- The drill can be expanded to allow two pitchers to oppose each other. They can alternate innings and keep score. For example, they can go five innings or 60 to 70 pitches each, whichever comes first.

102 GAME CONDITIONS

Objective: To improve the pitcher's concentration and selected mental aspects of pitching by simulating game conditions.

Equipment Needed: Gloves and baseballs.

Description: The drill involves three players. After properly warming up, the pitcher pitches a simulated game against a stand-in batter. The third player acts as the catcher. Every aspect of the simulated game is regulation, with the batter alternating as left- or right-handed hitters. The stand-in hitter protects himself by using his glove. If the ball is thrown too far inside, the batter catches it and gives it to the catcher. Prior to each pitch, the catcher gives the sign and location to the pitcher and sets up in his catching stance. The pitcher pitches his (simulated) game until he has thrown a prescribed number of innings or pitches as predetermined by his coach.

Coaching Points:

- Several baseballs should be available to conduct the drill, so that if a pitch gets past the catcher, the drill can be continued while the ball if being retrieved.
- Sufficient rest should be allotted between successive repetitions of the "game conditions" drills.

103 INTRA-SQUAD PRESSURE PITCHING

Objective: To provide pitchers with the opportunity to learn how to handle pressure situations they may have to face during the season.

Equipment Needed: Baseballs, gloves, bats, and bases.

Description: The team should be divided into two groups: one on offense and one on defense. The drill involves creating as many situations as possible with the offense trying to score and the defense trying to shut them out (late innings, ball-strike counts, runners on base, and ninth-inning jams). The pitcher has to pitch appropriately for each situation. The primary focus of the drill is to provide a competitive environment which allows pitchers to be better prepared for the season.

Coaching Points:

- The pitchers should not be overworked. As a general guideline, each pitcher should be limited to throw three to four innings maximum.
- The main emphasis of the drill is to create the "End Game."

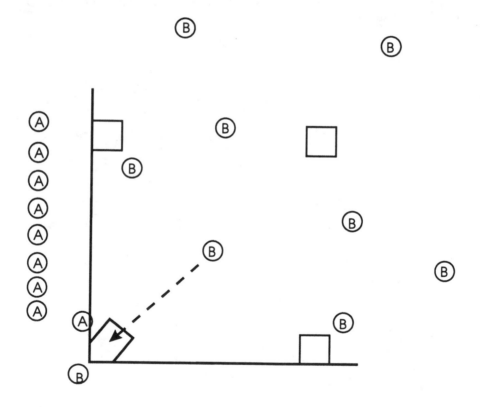

104 QUICK AS A CAT

Objective: To practice the basic mechanics of pitching quickly from the stretch position with a runner on first in a stealing situation. To teach the pitcher to throw quickly to either first or home.

Equipment Needed: Stopwatch, balls, and gloves.

Description: The basic focus of this drill is to develop maximum quickness in both a pitcher's delivery to home and his throws to first base. The general procedures for conducting the drill are relatively simple. Using a "glide step," the pitcher (A) delivers (throws) the baseball to home as quickly as he can, or fires the ball to the first baseman (B) as quickly as he can. His coach times the throws and calls out the times to him.

Coaching Points:

- A "good" time from the mound to the catcher is 1.3 seconds from the time the pitcher breaks his hands until the ball touches the catcher's mitt.
- A "good" time from the pitcher to first base is 1.1 seconds or better. A snap throw from a right-handed pitcher to first base is often as low as .9 or .8 seconds.
- The key for a right-handed pitcher is quick feet and short-arm movement. The key for a left-handed pitcher is quickness and deception.

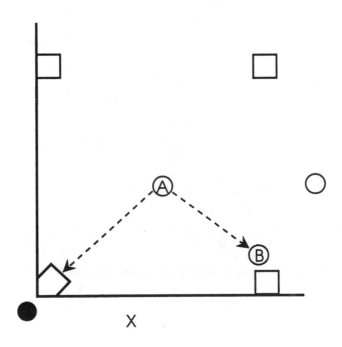

105 PEPPER – DOUBLE PLAY

Objective: To practice starting the 1-6-3 double play. To develop quick feet in the turn to second base. To practice making an accurate, chest-high throw to the middle infielders on the 1-6-3 double play.

Equipment Needed: A bat, baseballs, and gloves.

Description: The drill involves three players, all of which can be pitchers. One player (A) is the pitcher. A second player (B) serves as a hitter. The third player (C) acts as a middle infielder. The drill begins with player A pitching to B who is standing approximately 30 feet in front of him. Using a choke grip, player B attempts to hit a ground ball up the middle right back to A. Player A fields the ground ball, wheels, and throws to C who is standing at "second base" (approximately 40 feet behind A.) Player C then returns the ball to A, and the drill is continued. After 10 plays, the players rotate positions. The drill continues until each player has had 20 opportunities to make the play.

Coaching Points:

- The players should constantly be reminded to "speed up the drill."
- The emphasis should be on having a pitcher cleanly field the ground ball and then turn and make a strong, chest-high throw to second base.

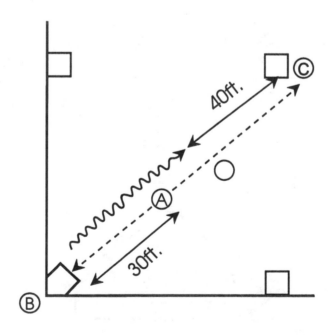

106 SITUATION PEPPER

Objective: To practice various situations in which the pitcher must cover first base and receive throws from either the first baseman or the second baseman (such as a bunt or double play).

Equipment Needed: Baseballs, a bat, and gloves.

Description: The drill involves four players: two pitchers (A and B), a first baseman (C), and a second baseman (D). One pitcher (A) throws from approximately a 30-foot distance to the other pitcher (B) who serves as a hitter. Player B hits a variety of ground balls to the right side of the infield or up the middle to A. Both player C and D assume positions in the field at their respective bases. The grounders hit by player B should be designated to create "game" situations for A. Player A should be forced to handle a variety of plays including bunts between the pitcher and the first baseman and 3-6-1 double plays. After a preset number of plays, player A and B switch roles.

Coaching Points:

- The bases can be shortened to make the drills move more rapidly.
- On bunt plays, the batter (B) calls the play (where to throw the ball) to player A.

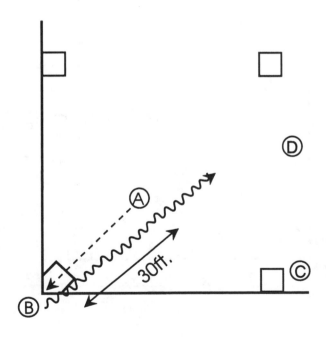

107 INFIELD PEPPER

Objective: To practice the skills and techniques required to respond to various infield ''game'' situations.

Equipment Needed: Baseballs, bats, and gloves.

Description: The drill involves using a complete infield to work on various infield situations. The bases are shortened to 75 feet. An extra pitcher serves as the batter. The coach calls out the play he wants (bunt situations, squeeze play situations, or double play situations, for example). From 35 to 40 feet, the pitcher delivers a soft throw to the batter who executes the play. The key to the drill is to keep the ball in the infield and to create every possible situation at some point during the drill. In most instances, the drill should be performed for approximately half an hour.

Coaching Points:

- If enough pitchers are available, they can hit the ball and run to first base, creating an even more gamelike situation.
- Variety can be incorporated into the drill by using outfielders as hitters and, subsequently, as baserunners.

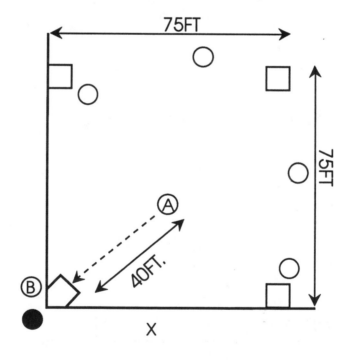

108 HAND PEPPER

Objective: To improve the pitcher's hand skills in fielding ground balls, particularly those that take difficult hops.

Equipment Needed: Baseballs and gloves.

Description: The drill involves two pitchers. The two players, standing approximately 12 to 15 feet apart, alternately try to throw the ball through their partner's legs. They throw one-hops, bad hops, and every other toss possible to challenge their partner. As a general rule, the drill should be performed for five minutes or less.

Coaching Points:

- Competition in the drill can be conducted by keeping track of the errors made. The player making the fewest errors is declared the winner.

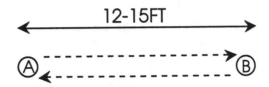

109 SITUATION PEPPER

Objective: To practice various situations (for example, bunts and double plays) on which the pitcher must cover first base and receive throws from either the first baseman or the second baseman.

Equipment Needed: Baseballs, a bat, and gloves.

Description: The drill involves four players: two pitchers (A and B), a first baseman (C), and a second baseman (D). One pitcher (A) throws from approximately a 30-foot distance to the other pitcher (B) who serves as a hitter. Player B hits a variety of ground balls to the right side of the infield or up the middle to A. Both player C and D assume positions in the field at their respective bases. The grounders hit by player B should be designed to create "game" situations for A. Player A should be forced to handle a variety of plays including bunts between the pitcher and the first baseman and 3-6-1 double plays. After a preset number of plays, players A and B switch roles.

Coaching Points:

- The bases can be shortened to make the drill move more rapidly.
- On bunt plays, the batter (B) calls the play (where to throw the ball) to player A.

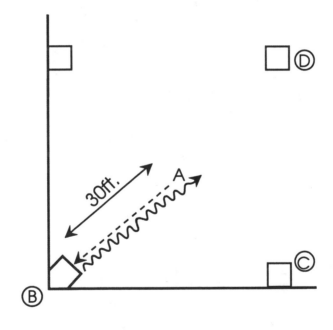

110 WALL PEPPER

Objective: To improve a pitcher's fielding techniques and skills; to enable a pitcher to develop "good hands."

Equipment Needed: Rubber balls of regulation size and weight and a wall.

Description: The drill involves one or more pitchers, each working alone. Each pitcher stands approximately 25 to 30 feet from the wall and throws a rubber ball against the wall so that the ball rebounds off the wall to create all sorts of ground balls. In his mind, the pitcher should envision a variety of baseball "game" situations. Depending on the simulated situation, he can then wheel back for the imaginary double play, field bunts, or throw to imaginary bases.

Coaching Points:

- The drill could also be conducted using two or more players simultaneously. One player could throw the ball off the wall and call out the "play." One of the other players would then field the ball off the wall.
- Traditionally, this is a very popular drill, particularly among kids in urban areas who have spent considerable time playing baseball in the streets.

111 "V" PICK-UPS

Objective: To improve lateral quickness, develop stamina, practice fielding, and work on the footwork involved in wheeling and throwing to a base.

Equipment Needed: Baseballs, gloves, and two cones.

Description: The drill involves two pitchers: one who serves in the field (A) and one who acts as a hitter (B). The two players stand 15 feet apart. A reasonable width is marked off with cones for player A to cover: approximately 10 feet to his right and 10 feet to his left. The drill begins by having player B firmly roll a baseball to A's right or left without letting A know which direction he's going to roll the ball. As the ball is rolled, player B calls out a base: first, second, third, or home. Player A then scoops up the ball, wheels and feigns a throw in the direction of the base which B called out. The thrower may also drop a bunt straight ahead and have player A charge, field the ball, and throw it where directed. The fielding pitcher should return to the middle of the two cones after every chance. After a preset number of chances, the two players exchange roles.

Coaching Points:

- The drill should be kept moving.
- The drill can be varied by adjusting either the distance between the players or between the cones.

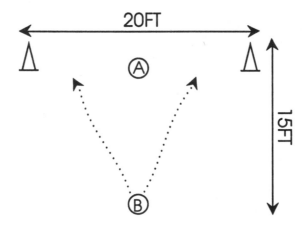

112 TWO-MAN PICK-OFFS

Objective: To practice accuracy, quickness, and footwork in pick-off throws to each base.

Equipment Needed: Baseballs and gloves.

Description: The drill involves having two pitchers work together on their pick-off throws at a distance of 45 to 50 feet. Each player concentrates on developing the proper footwork and making quick, accurate throws.

Coaching Points:

- This drill should be performed every day by the pitching staff.
- This drill can also be conducted without a ball in order to save the pitchers' arms, especially if they have pitched recently.

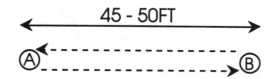

113   TEAM PICK-OFFS

Objective: To practice making strong, accurate throws. To involve the infielder on pick-off plays, and to work on solid team defense.

Equipment Needed: Baseballs and gloves.

Description: The drill involves a complete set of infielders: each at his position and four pitchers (A) positioned adjacent to the mound working at the same time delivering pick-off throws to each base. Each infielder works on his pick-off signs, moving to the bag to receive the throw, tagging, and returning the ball to the pitcher who threw him the ball. Home plate is treated as another first base station. The catcher acts as a first baseman. After six throws to each base, the players rotate. Depending on the number of pitchers available, at least two rounds of the drill should be performed.

Coaching Points:

- Good defensive teams practice pick-offs at each base until eventually they master the necessary techniques.
- Variation #1: Outfielders can be incorporated into the drill as lead-off runners; they should not attempt to return to the base on pick-off throws because of the potential of being hit with the throw.
- Variation #2: The drill can also be conducted without baseballs. This procedure can help save the pitchers' arms and allow baserunners to practice getting back to a base, or break for the next base, without the danger of being hit by the ball.

114 RIGHT SIDE PLAYS

Objective: To improve the ability of infielders to make plays on balls hit to the right side that require the pitcher to cover first.

Equipment Needed: Fungo bat, baseballs, and gloves.

Description: The drill involves a coach, a pitcher (A), and both right side infielders (the second baseman [B] and the first baseman [C]). The drill begins by having the coach hit fungo ground balls to the right side of the infield. The ball is fielded by either the first baseman or the second baseman. After the ball has been hit, the pitcher hustles to a specific aiming point where he catches the ball and tags the bag. The pitcher's aiming point is six to eight feet in front of the first base bag, slightly up the line. The pitcher stays inside the baseline, looking for the ball before he reaches the bag. He then tags the inside of the bag, while keeping his head down to make sure of the tag. After tagging the bag, he pivots back toward the center of the diamond to see if another runner is trying to advance a base.

Coaching Points:

- This drill requires both work and timing.
- The coach should occasionally lay down a drag bunt between the first baseman and the mound. Both the pitcher and the first baseman should go for the ball. If the pitcher fields the bunt, he should try to beat the runner to first base since he is aware of the fact that because the first baseman also went for the ball, he will not be in a position to cover the bag. On the other hand, if the first baseman fields the ball (because the ball went past the pitcher), he should then shovel the ball to the pitcher. The pitcher already has momentum toward the bag and is often in a reasonable position to beat the runner to first base.

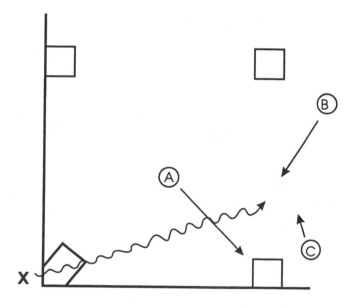

115   GLIDE STEP

Objective: To enable pitchers to develop quickness in throwing the ball either to home plate with a runner in stealing position or to first base.

Equipment Needed: Baseballs and gloves.

Description: The drill involves three pitchers. The pitchers form a triangle, approximately 45 feet apart. The drill begins by having the pitcher with the ball wheel and make a pick-off throw to home (to the player on his left in the triangle) or use a glide step and throw to home (to the player on his right in the triangle). The player who receives the throw then goes into his stretch and repeats the sequence of the drill (throwing either to first or home). Conducted on a continuous basis, the drill should be timed by the coach.

Coaching Points:

- The pitcher should be made aware of the importance of being able to throw quickly to both first base and home. He should be able to throw to first in one second or less. Although left-handed pitchers usually rely more on deceptiveness, they should be able to make a snap throw to first base in approximately one second.
- From the time the pitcher breaks his hands from the stretch position to the time the ball hits the catcher's glove, no more than 1.3 seconds should elapse. Such a goal can only be accomplished if the pitcher uses a good glide step.

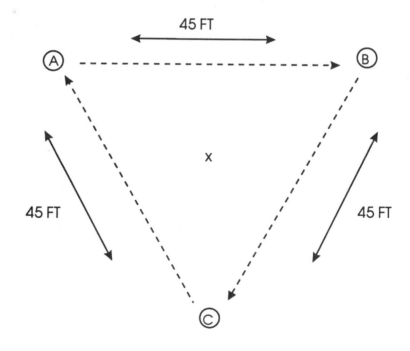

116 CALLING FOR THE POP-UP

Objective: To enable pitchers to practice handling pop flies in the infield and "calling out" the appropriate infielder to field a high pop fly which has been hit over the pitcher's mound.

Equipment Needed: Baseballs, gloves, and fungo bat.

Description: The drill involves a complete set of infielders, including the catcher, who are in position. The coach hits fungo pop-ups in the infield area, both fair and foul. Priorities are established, enabling decisions to be made on who will catch the ball. If a pop fly is hit above the mound, the pitcher calls who should take it.

Coaching Points:

- Pitchers must learn to make good judgments on pop flies.
- On short pop-ups, the pitcher may be in the best position to catch the ball. Accordingly, he should call out his own name and make the play.
- If the catcher loses the ball in the lights or the sun, the pitcher should be ready to make the catch.

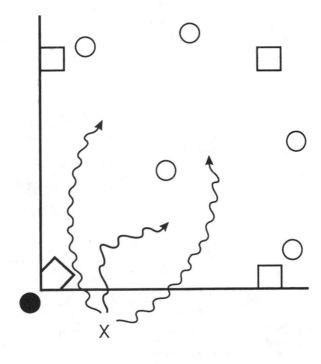

117 PASSED BALL

Objective: To practice receiving a throw from the catcher and applying a tag on the runner who is sliding in to home plate from third, without having the ball kicked out of the pitcher's glove. To enable catchers to practice making throws on short passed balls to pitchers who are covering home plate.

Equipment Needed: Baseballs and gloves.

Description: The drill involves two players: a pitcher and a catcher. Standing approximately 30 feet in front of the catcher, the pitcher throws the ball in the dirt to his catcher. The catcher allows the ball to get past him. The catcher then races after the ball, slides to it, quickly picks it up, and from his knees throws it to the pitcher who is covering the plate. The pitcher straddles the plate, leaving a portion of the plate "uncovered" for the runner to slide at. Upon catching the ball, the pitcher slaps a tag onto an imaginary runner. He then gets his glove hand up and out of the way of the runner as quickly as possible.

Coaching Points:

- The pitcher should be careful not to block the plate without the ball. A runner might bowl him over, an action that could result in a serious injury to the pitcher.
- The drill can be expanded by incorporating a baserunner. In this instance, the drill should be conducted on grass with the baserunner running at half-speed. Full-force collisions should be avoided at all costs.

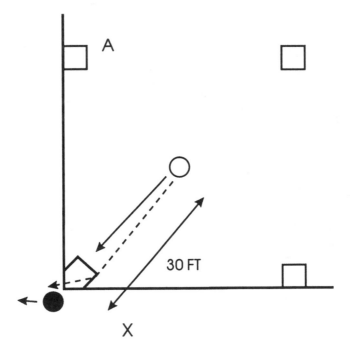

118 GLOVE POINT GAME

Objective: To improve a pitcher's control.

Equipment Needed: Baseballs, gloves, and moveable rubber home plates.

Description: The drill involves groups of three players: two pitchers and a catcher. The pitchers pair off, taking turns throwing to the catcher. The catcher gives five specific targets: high and low inside, both outside corners, and the center of the strike zone. The pitchers deliver the ball to the catcher's glove. Once he is able to repeatedly hit his target, the pitcher changes the type of pitch he is throwing (fastball, curve, or change-up) and continues throwing. The pitchers throw equal numbers of pitches from the windup and stretch positions.

Coaching Points:

- The drill can be varied to increase player interest by setting up a point system. Each pitcher receives one point per strike. The first player to earn 15 points wins. The catcher judges whether a pitch is a strike or not.
- The drill can also be made more difficult by eliminating the center of the strike zone, making it a "no-no" zone. As a result, only pitches on the corners count as strikes.
- Catchers should be reminded to give a clear target, holding their mitts steady. A moving target can create confusion and many cause the pitcher to lose his concentration.
- This drill can be performed either indoors or outdoors.

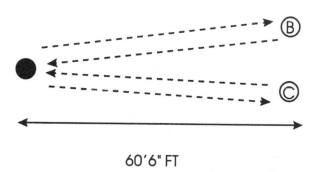

60'6" FT

5

OFFENSIVE DRILLS

Hitting

119 STRIDE DRILL

Objective: To practice properly striding while hitting.

Equipment Needed: Bats (one per player).

Description: The drill involves players working alone, practicing striding while hitting. As they practice, they are being critiqued by the coach. The drill begins by having the hitter assume his regular batting stance with a bat. On a self-pace basis, the hitter practices striding into the pitched ball. He isolates his stride by taking a relatively low, quick step forward. The coach makes individual corrections as needed.

Coaching Points:

- The coach should ensure that the hitter does not move his weight too far forward during his stride because such an action will cause the hitter's hips to be thrown forward.

120 HIP TURN DRILL

Objective: To practice opening the hips while hitting. To develop the ability to rotate the hips faster. To improve quickness while swinging the bat (particularly on inside pitches). To gain an appreciation for the relationship of hip speed to the entire swing.

Equipment Needed: Bats (or substitute items), and gloves.

Description: The drill involves players working alone on improving their ability to open their hips while hitting. As they practice, they are being critiqued by the coach. The drill begins by having the hitter place a bat (or the substitute item) behind his back at waist level. Keeping the bat horizontal to the ground, the hitter holds on to the back side of the bat so that he can pull hard while performing the drill. He uses his glove as home plate. The hitter assumes his regular batting stance and then "watches" an imaginary pitch being thrown to him. Initially, the drill is performed without having the hitter stride. In this instance, the hitter takes a position as though he has completed striding. As the imaginary pitch is delivered, he pulls the bat with his dominant hand so that the head of the bat is pointed towards the pitcher. At the same time, he is opening his hips, he rolls up on his back foot. Once the basic techniques have been mastered, the hitter practices striding into the imaginary pitch, while simultaneously opening his hips and pulling on the bat. He uses the bat to help his hips drive through the pitch.

Coaching Points:

- The coach should make sure that the hitter pivots on the ball of his rear foot.
- This drill should be part of every hitter's daily regimen.

121 HIP THRUST DRILL

Objective: To practice thrusting the hips while hitting. To develop the ability to roll up on the rear foot while swinging. To improve the hitter's ability to properly use his hips while hitting.

Equipment Needed: Bats and gloves.

Description: The drill involves players working alone on improving their ability to effectively utilize their hips while hitting. Each player uses his glove as home plate. The drill begins by having each player (hitter) place a bat on or slightly off his shoulder. The player assumes his regular batting stance and then "watches" an imaginary pitch being thrown to him. When the imaginary pitch gets close to home plate, he visualizes either hitting it to the opposite field or pulling it to the power field. As the ball "arrives," the batter rotates his hips instead of swinging. He then rolls up on his back foot and thrusts his hips through the ball – thereby placing his body in position to help his hands drive his bat through the hitting zone.

Coaching Points:

- This drill should be performed daily.
- Variety can be added to the drill by having the hitter perform a preset number of thrusts as if hitting first to the opposite field and then to the power field. Finally, he should swing away.

122 LEAD ARM EXTENSION DRILL

Objective: To practice properly extending the lead arm while hitting.

Equipment Needed: Bats and gloves.

Description: The drill involves players working alone on improving their lead arm extension while hitting. Each player uses his glove as home plate. The drill begins by having each player (hitter) assumes his regular batting stance with his front (lead) hand on the bat and his back hand placed behind his back. The hitter then takes a (form) swing using only his lead hand. The coach checks the hitter to ensure that he has properly extended his lead arm.

Coaching Points:

- The drill can be varied by using the back hand on the bat instead of the lead hand.
- Depending on the strength and size of the hitter, some players may either use a lighter (than normal) bat or choke up on the bat while performing this drill.

123 WRIST ROLLER

Objective: To improve bat speed and bat control, and to develop maximum efficiency and power in the swing.

Equipment Needed: Bats (one per player).

Description: The drill involves players working alone on improving both bat speed and bat control. The drill begins by having each player (hitter) assume the contact-the-ball (mid-swing) position. Keeping his hands and wrists relaxed, he then rolls the bat forward and backward in such a way as to touch each of his shoulders as it completes a full arc. He uses only his wrists and forearms to rotate the bat. Throughout the drill, he keeps his hips facing the imaginary pitcher.

Coaching Points:

- The drill should be performed quickly and continuously (60 to 80 repetitions) for approximately one minute.
- The drill can be varied by having the hitter begin the drill in his regular batting stance and then swing at an imaginary pitch, while extending his elbows quickly to promote bat speed and bat control.

124 STAYING BACK CHAIR DRILL

Objective: To have the hitter practice keeping his rear leg back while swinging the bat. To ensure that the hitter's front side does not leave too soon during the swing.

Equipment Needed: A bat and a folding chair.

Description: The drill involves players working alone on improving their ability to keep their rear legs back while swinging the bat. The drill begins by having the hitter assume his regular batting stance with his back leg pressed against a folding chair. He then practices swinging a bat against an imaginary pitch. After each swing, he checks to see how much space he has between his leg and the chair. If his body left too soon on the swing, there will be a relatively large space between his hip and the chair.

Coaching Points:

- A hitter must learn to stay back and hit off his back side if he hopes to hit with any power.
- The drill can be expanded by having the hitter actually swing at a rubber ball thrown by another player.

125 SWINGING DOWNWARD CHAIR DRILL

Objective: To practice the proper mechanics of the swing and develop the ability not to uppercut while swinging.

Equipment Needed: A bat, a folding chair, and a batting tee.

Description: The drill involves players working alone on teaching the proper hitting stroke, particularly the ability to swing down through the ball. The drill begins by having the hitter assume his regular batting stance next to a folding chair with the seat facing forward. In front of the chair, a batting tee is set (positioned just slightly lower than the back of the chair) with a ball placed on the tee. The drill requires the hitter to swing at the ball without hitting the chair. In order to perform the drill properly, the batter must swing with a slightly downward angle. If the hitter does not take a slightly downward plane with his swing, he will hit the chair. The drill is designed to force hitters to concentrate on using the correct bat angle.

Coaching Points:

- This drill is excellent for teaching players what type of stroke they need for hitting specific types of balls (grounders, line drives, etc.).
- This drill should be performed at least a couple of times per week.

126 BACK-SIDE FUNGOES

Objective: To practice the mechanics of the proper downswing while hitting and learn how to stay back while swinging the bat. To help teach hitting the other way.

Equipment Needed: A fungo bat, several dozen tennis balls, and a net.

Description: The drill involves players working alone on the mechanics of hitting. Using a bucket of tennis balls and a fungo bat, the batter hits balls into the netting. The drill begins by having the batter flip the ball into the air with his back hand (not his front hand). Using his back hand to flip the ball is designed to remind the player to hit off of his back side. Prior to swinging at the ball, he should visualize hitting different types of pitches to different locations on the field. For example, if he wants to hit hard ground balls to the shortstop, he should remind himself to stay on top of the ball and swing at it once the ball falls to a point somewhere in the area between chest high and his belly button. He follows the same procedures for hitting a "high fastball." On the other hand, if he wants to practice hitting the ball to the opposite side, he should position his body to hit that direction into the net (attack the ball off of his back hip while keeping his bat angle at 45 degrees from his body).

Coaching Points:

- The hitter should be reminded that he may feel awkward for awhile until he has mastered the technique of using the back of his hand to flip the ball.
- It is recommended that this drill should be performed daily at practice. As a rule, approximately 100 repetitions should be done: 50 high pitches and 50 pitches to the opposite field.

127 OVERLOAD DRILL

Objective: To practice the proper mechanics of hitting, particularly how to keep the front shoulder in as long as possible. To teach the hitter to keep his head down while swinging. To develop the ability to hit line drives and ground balls to the opposite field.

Equipment Needed: Baseballs, gloves, and bats (one per player).

Description: The drill involves a four-step procedure which is performed by three players: a hitter, a player who pitches to him, and a catcher. In step one, the batter assumes a perpendicular hitting position. His rear foot is approximately four to six inches from home plate. His front foot is parallel to his rear foot in a line which is perpendicular to the plate. His chest is facing the pitcher. The drill begins by having the pitcher throw pitches to the hitter. The hitter swings at the pitches without moving his feet. He can swivel his hips and turn his front shoulder, but he cannot stride or roll up on his back foot. The emphasis is for the hitter to keep his shoulder in and his head down while attempting to hit to the opposite field. In step two, the procedures are the same except that the hitter changes the position of each foot slightly. He rotates his rear foot a bit toward the catcher and moves his front foot to an angle up the line (the third baseline for right-handed hitters; the first baseline for left-handed hitters). Similar to step one, the pitcher feeds the hitter pitches. The hitter swings at the pitches but is not allowed to move his feet. In step three, the hitter assumes his regular hitting stance. The coach or one of the other players calls out "stride." Without committing his hand, the hitter takes his normal stride toward home plate and stops. The pitcher then feeds him the ball. Keeping his front shoulder closed, the hitter swings and attempts to hit the ball hard to the opposite field. He completes his swing by rolling up on his back foot. The procedures for step four are the same as for step three except that there is no stopping. The hitter takes a full swing.

128 SHORT STRIDE SPIN DRILL

Objective: To help hitters practice the proper mechanics of hitting and eliminate their problems with their swing. To develop the feeling of being balanced and comfortable while swinging.

Equipment Needed: Baseballs, gloves, and bats.

Description: The drill involves three players: a hitter (A), a catcher, and a player to feed pitches to the batter. The hitter assumes his regular hitting position. The drill begins by having the coach or another player call out a code word ("spin" or "stride," for example) to the hitter. The hitter then takes a relatively short stride (approximately four inches) at a 45-degree angle toward home plate, stepping gingerly on the big toe of his lead (striding) foot. At that point, the feeder tosses a pitch to the hitter. The hitter swings at the ball, rolling up on his rear foot and thrusting his hips forward. Maintaining his balance throughout the swing, the batter attempts to hit the ball hard.

Coaching Points:

- This drill is particularly valuable for hitters who overstride, drop their hands, tend to lunge at pitches, tend to step into the bucket, have difficulty hitting to the opposite field, or make improper use of their rear foot or hips while swinging.

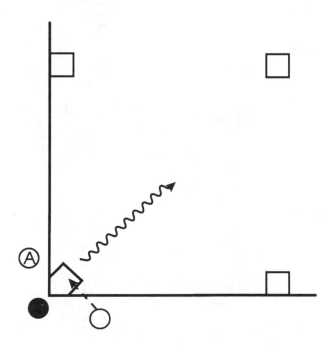

129   HITTING THE HIGH PITCH

Objective: To practice hitting pitches in the top of the strike zone.

Equipment Needed: Baseballs, a bat, and a hitting tee.

Description: The drill involves players working alone on practicing hitting the high pitch. The baseball is placed on a tee which has been raised to a point where the ball is in the top of the hitter's strike zone. The drill begins by having the hitter who is in his regular hitting stance take his normal stride and his normal swing. (Note: The hitter does not flex his front knee.) The hitter focuses on the proper mechanics for hitting the high pitch. He swings slightly down through the ball. He takes the shortest route to the high pitch by leading his swing at the ball with the knob of his bat and pulling his hands down and across his body. Finally, he attempts to hit the ball hard and on a line.

Coaching Points:

- If the hitter hits underneath the ball, he will miss the ball completely and hit the tee (a telltale sign of a serious problem with his swing).
- If necessary, the hitting tee can be raised by placing blocks of wood underneath it.

130 SHORT SCREEN STRIKES

Objective: To practice the proper mechanics of hitting under favorable conditions and increase the number of swings a batter can receive during hitting practice.

Equipment Needed: Baseballs, a bat, and a screen.

Description: The drill involves players working alone on the proper hitting mechanics. Kneeling on one knee behind a short screen which is positioned approximately 20 to 30 feet in front of the hitter, the coach throws practice pitches to the hitter. The increased proximity to the hitter provided by the short screen allows the coach to better control where he throws the ball. As a result, he can throw more strikes. The hitter has more pitches in the strike zone at which to swing (practice). The hitter will not have to spend time having to avoid errant pitches. The coach can throw pitches to the specific locations the hitter needs to practice. Collectively, the drill helps to maximize the hitter's practice time.

Coaching Points:

- The coach should critique the hitter's adherence to proper hitting mechanics.
- This drill enables batting practice pitchers to target specific locations with relatively great accuracy.

131 NOW DRILL

Objective: To develop the ability to wait on pitches before swinging. To develop a feel for how long a hitter should wait on pitches thrown to specific locations before starting his swing.

Equipment Needed: Baseballs, a bat, and gloves.

Description: The drill involves three players: a hitter, a pitcher, and a catcher. The hitter faces pitches being thrown from regulation distance. On the first several pitches, the hitter does not swing at the ball. Instead, he visualizes hitting the ball hard to the opposite field. As the pitch is being delivered, the hitter waits until the ball gets so close he feels that he can't wait any longer to swing at the pitch and still hit it to the opposite field. At that precise moment, he yells "Now" instead of swinging. This technique is designed to teach him physically where the ball is when his swing would begin. After practicing and visualizing several "now" pitches, the hitter then swings away and attempts to hit the ball to the opposite field. The hitter should gain an appreciation for the fact that although his swing is exactly the same for both an outside and an inside pitch, he must wait a split second longer before hitting an outside pitch to the opposite field.

Coaching Points:

- In general, the hitter who waits to hit a ball to the opposite field should wait until an outside pitch is approximately 4 to 8 inches from the plate before swinging; on inside pitches, he should wait until the pitch is 2 to 3 feet in front of the plate.
- If he knows where the ball should be when he starts his swing, the hitter will have a better feel for the timing of his swing.

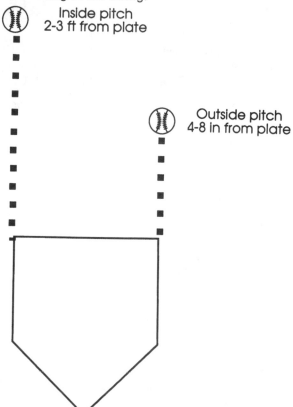

Inside pitch
2-3 ft from plate

Outside pitch
4-8 in from plate

132 HITTER'S CHOICE

Objective: To develop the ability for a batter to hit the ball where he wants, either on the ground or in the air.

Equipment Needed: Baseballs, a bat, and gloves.

Description: The drill involves three players: a hitter, a pitcher, and a catcher. The drill is designed to teach hitters how to hit pitches on the ground or in the air without adjusting their batting strokes. If the hitter wants to hit a ground ball, he attempts to hit the top half of the ball. On the other hand, if he wants to hit a fly ball, he attempts to hit the bottom half of the ball. The pitcher throws balls to various locations, and the hitter tries to hit either the top or the bottom half of the ball.

Coaching Points:

- The drill emphasizes the fact to the hitter that he must change his target, not his stance or his stroke, in order to hit a specific type of ball (a grounder or a fly ball).
- This drill is for relatively accomplished hitters who have already mastered the basic fundamentals of hitting.

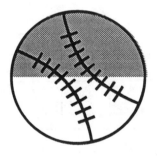

To hit a ground ball, target your eyes on the top half of the ball.

To hit a fly ball, target your eyes on the bottom half of the ball.

133 PROPER CONTACT POINT

Objective: To practice the proper mechanics of the swing; to develop bat control.

Equipment Needed: Baseballs, gloves, a home plate, bats, a batting helmet, and a fence (or a net).

Description: The drill involves players working in pairs. One player (A) acts as the hitter, while the other player (B) serves as the tosser. The hitter stands approximately 10 to 15 feet in front of a fence. The tosser stands slightly to one side of the hitter and tosses balls to the hitter. Each toss is aimed in the direction of a specific contact area of the plate (the plate is divided into three specific areas: left side, middle, and right side). Every few seconds, the tosser tosses a new ball to a different contact point. The batter hits each toss at the specific contact point into the fence. On each swing, the hitter strives for proper bat control. During the drill, the tosser wears a batting helmet for safety purposes. The tosser also provides feedback to the hitter regarding the hitter's adherence to proper hitting mechanics.

Coaching Points:

- The hitter can perform this drill using either both hands or one hand (lead or back hand) on the bat while swinging.
- After a preset number of swings (25), the players switch roles.

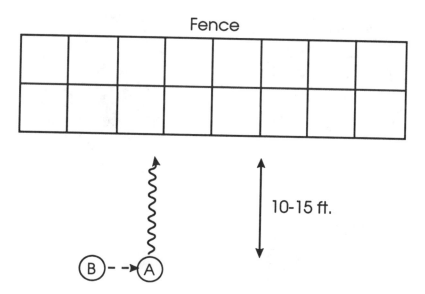

134 MULTIPLE FINGERS DRILL

Objective: To improve a hitter's visual tracking system.

Equipment Needed: A glove (to serve as home plate).

Description: The drill involves two players. One player (A) assumes a kneeling position approximately two feet in front of home plate. His primary responsibility is to pass his hand through the strike zone and to show a varying number of fingers as he moves his hand. The other player (B) simulates swinging a bat without actually using a bat. As he performs his simulated swings, he attempts to closely adhere to the proper mechanics of the hitting stroke. Player B must also keep his head down and watch (track) A's hand as it passes through the strike zone and loudly call out the number of fingers Player A is showing when A's hand is in the strike zone. Player A critiques B's swing and provides corrective feedback as needed.

Coaching Points:

- A good hitter can concentrate on both the proper mechanics of hitting and properly tracking the pitch simultaneously.
- Hitters should look for possible cues before the pitcher releases the ball, which may aid them in tracking the ball.
- Visual discipline is a critical factor in being a successful hitter.

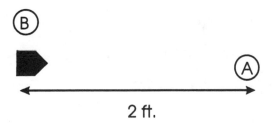

2 ft.

135 KEEPING YOUR EYE ON THE BALL

Objective: To practice keeping proper eye contact with the ball.

Equipment Needed: Gloves, baseballs, a bat, and a home plate.

Description: The drill involves three-player groups (a hitter [A], a pitcher [B], and a catcher). As many groups can participate in the drill as space permits or the situation dictates. The hitter assumes his regular batting position at home plate. The pitcher stands approximately 30 to 40 feet in front of the hitter. The catcher is in a catching position behind home plate. The drill requires the hitter to closely watch each pitch from the moment the pitcher releases it until it reaches the hitter's contact point. After a few pitches in which the hitter has demonstrated that he can keep his head down while visually tracking the ball, the hitter should then call out a cue word (for example, "Now," "Go," or "Yes,") to signify when he should swing at the ball. Another option would be to have the hitter call out the type of pitch thrown to him (for example, high fastball, low curve ball, or split-fingered fastball).

Coaching Points:

- The drill should emphasize maintaining eye contact with the ball.
- Depending on the coach's philosophy, the pitcher could be allowed to watch (track) the ball from its release point all the way into the catcher's glove.

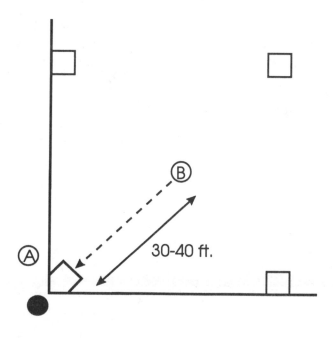

30-40 ft.

136 SWEEPING-SWING WALL DRILL

Objective: To practice the proper mechanics of the hitting stroke. To correct the faulty habits of a hitter who has a "sweeping swing."

Equipment Needed: A bat, a Gillespie power hitting vest, and a wall or a fence.

Description: The drill involves players working alone on overcoming the hitting fault of having a "sweeping swing." The drill requires the hitter (with a bat) to assume his regular batting stance facing the wall which is only 36 inches away. He then practices his normal batting swing and tries not to hit the wall with his bat. If he uses a "sweeping swing," he will hit the wall with his bat. As a result, with the wall as an obstruction, he must learn to keep his hands inside and tight to his body during the swing. If he keeps his hands in the proper position, he will increase his bat speed. He will also be better able to hit the inside pitch with the "fat" part of his bat. During the early stages of this drill, the hitter should wear a Gillespie hitting vest in order to ensure that he swings the bat through the proper plane.

Coaching Points:

- A "sweeping swing" will cause a hitter to hit inside pitches on the handle of the bat (instead of the thick part of the bat).
- A "sweeping swing" slows down the speed of the bat.

137 LOOPING-SWING WALL DRILL

Objective: To practice the proper mechanics of the hitting stroke. To correct the faulty habits of a hitter who has a "looping swing."

Equipment Needed: A bat, a Gillespie power hitting vest, and a wall or a fence.

Description: The drill involves players working alone on overcoming the hitting fault of having a "looping swing." The drill requires the hitter (with a bat) to stand at a 90-degree angle to the wall, with his rear foot twelve inches from the wall. Facing a "phantom" pitcher, he assumes his regular hitting stance and attempts to hit an imaginary pitch. If he has a loop in his swing, his bat will hit the wall. As a result, with the wall as an obstruction, he must learn to shorten his swing and avoid the bad habit of looping his bat during his swing. If he makes the necessary adjustments in his swing, he will increase his bat speed. He will also be better able to get on top of a high fastball. During the early stages of this drill, the hitter should wear a Gillespie hitting vest in order to provide him with the correct "feel" for swinging the bat through the proper plane.

Coaching Points:

- A long, "looping swing" will result in a hitter's taking longer to get his bat on the ball, making it more likely that the hitter will either miss the ball or be late on the pitch.
- Hitters who have a "looping swing" have trouble with high fastballs.

138 SPOT THE TEE WORK

Objective: To practice the proper mechanics of hitting. To develop the swing me-chanics required for hitting a ball to a specific location. To teach the hitter the proper bat angle to drive the ball to the opposite field, as well as the proper bat angle for pulling the high, inside corner fastball.

Equipment Needed: A bat, baseballs (or tennis balls), a batting tee, and a net.

Description: The drill involves players working alone on practicing the mechanics of hitting a baseball at various locations. The drill requires a hitter to hit the ball off a batting tee into a net. The ball is set on the tee which has been set at a height which will require the batter to use a specific bat angle when swinging. For example, in order to hit the ball to the opposite field, the batter must hit the ball off his back hip, which requires a bat angle of 45 degrees from his body. In order to pull a high-and-tight pitch, the batter must make contact well in front of home plate, which requires a bat angle of 75 to 80 degrees from his body. Once the batter decides where he wants to hit the ball, he should first envision an imaginary pitcher releasing the ball and then proceed to hit the ball off the tee. He should ensure that his stride foot is on the ground well before his bat contacts the ball.

Coaching Points:

- A common fault of batters hitting the ball off the tee is that they have their stride foot in the air as contact with the ball is made.
- The hitter must work on "pitch location" on every swing and must attack the ball using the proper swing for a particular location.
- Working on "pitch location" on every swing requires intense concentration and focus.

139 1-2-3 TEE WORK

Objective: To practice proper batting mechanics. To provide a methodical, repetitive means for correcting faults in the execution of the proper techniques of the swing.

Equipment Needed: Baseballs (or tennis balls), a bat, a batting tee, and a net.

Description: The drill involves players working alone on practicing the proper mechanics of hitting. The drill requires a hitter to hit balls off a batting tee into a net. The hitter performs the drill in a three-step sequential fashion. First, he assumes his regular hitting stance an appropriate distance away from a hitting tee on which a baseball has been placed. Next, he initiates the swing by taking an inward turn and a good stride (a short stride at approximately a 45-degree angle toward home plate). Finally, he simultaneously rolls up on his back foot and thrusts his hips and swings. The drill is designed to provide the hitter with the means for developing good hitting habits: the proper positioning of his rear foot during the normal batting stroke, and a proper stride. Once the hitter has gained a relative mastery of the skills involved in the three-step process, he should then take live cuts at the ball off the tee.

Coaching Points:

- All factors considered, this drill offers a more effective means for correcting hitting faults than swinging incorrectly at live pitching.
- The hitter can break the mechanics of the drill down by first using only one hand on the bat while swinging (either his lead hand or his back hand) and, subsequently, using both hands.

140 INWARD TURN DRILL

Objective: To develop the ability to make an inward turn (going back before going forward to figuratively "load" the bat) while hitting. To practice coiling like a spring, gathering strength, and then uncoiling.

Equipment Needed: Baseballs, a bat, and gloves.

Description: The drill involves three players (a hitter, a catcher, and a pitcher). Both the catcher and the pitcher assume their normal positions in the field. The hitter gets into his regular hitting stance. The drill requires the hitter to begin moving slightly back and forth (from the pitcher to the catcher and so on) once he's in his hitting stance. Basically, the movement is performed in rhythmic fashion, lifting his heels from the ground one at a time, and shifting his weight from one side to the other. The focus of the drill is to make an inward turn easier as a result of the hitter's rhythmic movement. As the hitter moves, he is required to call out a "1-2-3-4" count to signify the four steps involved in making an inward turn. On "one," he rocks (moves) toward the pitcher. On "two," he rocks back toward the catcher. On "three," he rocks toward the pitcher again. Finally, on "four," he rocks toward the catcher again, coils his hands, and explodes into his swing. The front half of the hitter's body (the front knee, the front hip, and the front shoulder) are involved in coiling the hitter's hands. The pitcher begins throwing the ball on the hitter's "three" count. As a result, when the hitter rocks back on "four," the ball will be on its way to the plate, thereby making the hitter's timing just about right.

141 MIRROR DRILL

Objective: To provide the means for having a hitter review and evaluate his own hitting mechanics; to practice shadow hitting.

Equipment Needed: A bat and a full-length mirror.

Description: Using a full-length mirror, the hitter positions himself either sideways facing the mirror or front-on looking at the mirror as though the mirror is the "pitcher." Assuming his regular hitting stance, the hitter initially checks out how well he sets up and gets ready to hit. He then swings at a series of imaginary pitches, hypothetically thrown to all locations of the strike zone. While he's swinging, he checks out his adherence to the proper mechanics of the swing (for example, body position, weight distribution, proper balance, inward turn, striding, and stroke mechanics).

Coaching Points:

- This drill should be performed daily or on an as-needed basis, 40 to 50 swings per session.
- This drill could be further enhanced through the use of a video camera.
- The hitter should concentrate on a variety of pitch locations when taking his swings at imaginary pitches, particularly those locations which may be giving him specific problems in a game.

142 PERSONALIZED STRIKE ZONE SWINGS

Objective: To develop and enhance a hitter's tracking system: a system which involves the collective ability to determine the speed, rotation, and proper contact point of each pitch.

Equipment Needed: A bat, a poster (or banner) which illustrates the batter's personal strike zone, and a three-area home plate.

Description: The drill involves players working alone on developing their tracking system to monitor each pitch while it is being delivered. The drill can be performed outdoors or indoors. A poster (or banner) which illustrates the batter's personal strike zone is hung on a wall (or fence). The multi-colored home plate with each color designating a specific part of the strike zone, the inside, outside, and middle of the plate, is placed in front of the poster. The drill requires the hitter to take his regular batting stance next to home plate and visualize that a specific type of pitch (fastball, curve, slider, for example) has been thrown to a specific location within his personal strike zone (for example, high and inside or low and outside). The hitter then hypothesizes a specific game situation and visualizes the path of the ball that he envisions he would be thrown in that setting. In the initial stages of this drill, the hitter also visualizes the swing he would take at that pitch (he does not actually swing a bat at this point in the drill). Subsequently, he would incorporate live swings into the drill.

Coaching Points:

- A mirror could be added to the drill after the hitter has mastered the basic techniques involved in the drill.

STRIKE
ZONE

143 CHECK-ME-OUT DRILL

Objective: To have the coach or another player check out the hitting mechanics of the batter.

Equipment Needed: A bat.

Description: The coach stands approximately eight to ten feet in front of the batter who is in his regular hitting stance. After initiating the drill by calling out "ready," the coach points to a specific spot in the hitter's strike zone. At that moment, the batter swings at the imaginary pitch thrown to that spot. The coach critiques the hitter's mechanics.

Coaching Points:

- The coach should point to a wide variety of locations within the hitter's strike zone.
- If the hitter has a mechanical flaw in his swing at pitches thrown to a particular spot in his strike zone, the coach should require the hitter to spend additional time on that specific location.

144 ONE-HAND SWING

Objective: To teach (and practice) the hitting mechanics of swinging slightly downward while hitting.

Equipment Needed: Baseballs, a bat, a home plate, and a short screen.

Description: The drill involves two players: a hitter and someone who is acting as a pitcher. The hitter assumes his regular batting stance except for the fact he holds on to the bat with one hand. He places whatever hand is not on the bat across his chest. The hand holding the bat is choked up to the top of the tape (or grip) on the bat. Kneeling on one knee behind a short screen, the pitcher throws to the hitter from approximately 20 to 30 feet away. The hitter uses a lighter or shorter bat to lessen the strain on his wrists and shoulders. The coach requires the hitter to pull his hips through the swing and to emphasize using a slightly downward swing. After a preset number of repetitions while holding and swinging the bat only with his top hand, the hitter switches and uses only his bottom hand for five repetitions.

Coaching Points:

- The drill can be varied by having the hitter perform the drill from a kneeling position.
- The drill can have a positive effect on the hitter's confidence in his ability to make contact with the ball while swinging.

145 CALL-THE-PITCH FLIP DRILL

Objective: To practice the proper hitting mechanics. To enable the hitter to get the maximum number of swings in the shortest amount of time. To develop the ability to hit balls pitched (flipped) to various locations.

Equipment Needed: A bat, a home plate, a net, and a bucket of tennis balls.

Description: The drill involves two players: a hitter (A) and a flipper (B) (someone who flips balls to the batter to hit). The hitter assumes his regular batting stance. The flipper kneels on one knee, 10 to 12 feet in front of and slightly off to the dominant side (the right side for a right-handed hitter, and vice-versa) of the hitter. The flipper calls out the location and the speed of the pitch (for example, a high fastball) and then flips the (tennis) ball to the location he called out. For a preset number of repetitions, the batter works on his hitting mechanics for swinging at balls in that location. After the batter has hit approximately 25 flips, the players switch roles. The drill continues by varying the "location" of the flipped balls until each hitter has taken a total of about a hundred swings.

Coaching Points:

- Variety can be added to the drill by having the flipper not give the location or the speed of the ball, thereby requiring the hitter to react to the "pitch" cold-turkey.

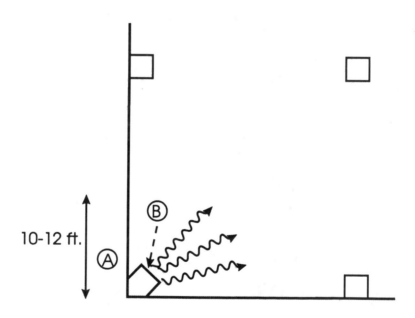

146 GAME-CONDITION, TWO-STRIKE HITTING

Objective: To teach the mechanics of hitting with a two-strike count (for example, choking up on the bat). To emphasize the importance of not striking out.

Equipment Needed: Baseballs, bases, bats, and gloves.

Description: The drill involves dividing the team into two groups (A and B) for intra-squad competition. Competition is conducted under game-type conditions with regular baseball rules (for example, live pitching, hitting, and defense) with one exception: every hitter has two strikes on him when he gets in the batter's box. If he strikes out twice during the game, he can't bat again until the next game begins. He can play defense, but he loses his turn at bat. The team that strikes out the least wins the game.

Coaching Points:

- The importance of protecting the plate (by choking up on the bat and watching the ball) is emphasized.
- The coach critiques the hitting mechanics of the batter.

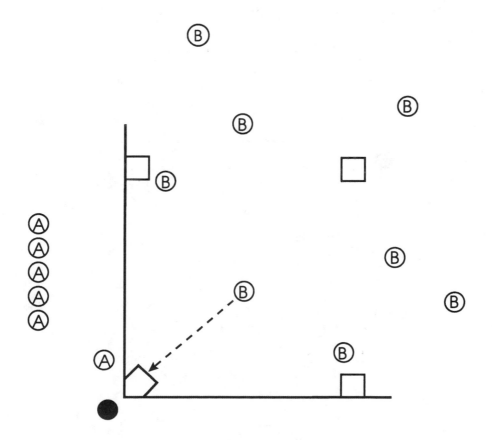

147   HITTING THE OPPOSITE WAY — THREE-MAN PEPPER

Objective: To teach bat control. To practice the mechanics of hitting behind the runner, and to develop the ability to hit the ball the opposite way.

Equipment Needed: Baseballs, gloves, and a bat.

Description: The drill involves three players: a hitter (A), a pitcher (B), and a fielder (C). The hitter assumes his regular batting stance. The pitcher is approximately 25 to 30 feet in front of the hitter. The third player, the fielder, is positioned at a 45-degree angle approximately 20 feet from the hitter (to the hitter's right for right-handed batters; to the hitter's left for left-handed swingers). The drill begins by having the pitcher throw firmly and accurately to the hitter who attempts to hit a one-hopper the other direction to the fielder. The fielder catches the ball and quickly returns it to the pitcher. The pitcher then throws another ball to the hitter, and the drill continues. After a preset number of pitches, the players rotate.

Coaching Points:

- The drill is designed to help the batter learn how to drive the ball on the ground, a basic skill for being able to "hit and run."

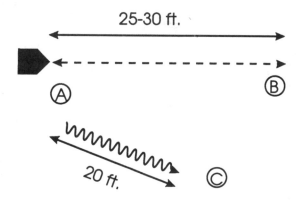

148 SOFT-TOSS SUPER-FOCUS DRILL

Objective: To practice the proper hitting mechanics. To develop the ability to wait on a pitch before swinging.

Equipment Needed: Baseballs, a bat, a home plate, and a screen.

Description: The drill involves two players: a hitter and a feeder (someone to toss the ball to the hitter, this person can be another player or a coach). The hitter assumes his regular batting stance. The feeder assumes a kneeling position, five to six feet behind and to the side of the hitter (to the right for right-handed hitters, to the left for left-handed hitters). The drill begins by having the feeder toss pitches to the hitter from the feeder's position behind the hitter so that the ball comes up "through" the strike zone. The hitter is forced to wait on the ball before swinging. Keeping his hands back until the last possible second, the hitter sees the ball out of the corner of his eye and then swings through the hitting zone attempting to drive the ball into the screen.

Coaching Points:

- The hitter should concentrate on keeping his hands back and delaying his hitting stroke as long as possible.
- The hitter should keep his head down, focused on the hitting zone; he should not turn and look at the feeder.
- This drill is particularly useful for learning how to wait on breaking pitches.

149 PASSED BALL

Objective: To practice the proper mechanics of hitting. To work on hitting low pitches.

Equipment Needed: Baseballs, a bat, and a hitting tee.

Description: The drill involves players working alone on their hitting mechanics by practicing hitting balls off a hitting tee. The tee is adjusted so that it is knee high (or slightly below knee high) to the hitter. The tee is then positioned on the outside edge of home plate, and a ball is placed on the tee in order to give the batter the opportunity to practice hitting a pitch that has been "thrown" low and outside. Assuming his regular hitting stance, the batter swings and hits the ball. During his swing, he should go down as far as necessary to "get" the ball by flexing his knees. He should not alter his bat angle in order to hit the ball. After completing his swing and follow-through, the hitter should immediately kneel down and touch his back knee on the ground. If he can't do this, he was off balance while swinging (he probably was not in the proper position to hit the ball).

Coaching Points:

- Variety can be added to the drill by subsequently moving the tee to other positions (the middle and the inside of home plate).
- On outside low pitches, the hitter should visualize hitting the ball on the ground to the opposite field; more often than not, the player will then hit a line drive.

150 TASK AT HAND DRILL

Objective: To provide the hitter with the opportunity to practice hitting under various game-time situations. To develop a hitter's sense of confidence about being able to handle a particular game-time situation.

Equipment Needed: Baseballs and a bat.

Description: The drill involves having a hitter (A) practice hitting while facing a variety of counts and situations. The hitter faces either live pitching or a pitching machine. The coach calls out the count and the tactical situation (for example, zero to two count, runners on first and third, two outs, and others) The batter reacts accordingly. For example, on zero to two counts, the batter must protect the plate regardless of the type of pitch and the situation. The coach continually varies the game-time challenge the hitter must face. By forcing the hitter to deal with and handle each challenge successfully, the drill is designed to enhance the hitter's mental toughness.

Coaching Points:

- The drill can be varied by eliminating the counts and just having the hitter confront specific situations (for example, hit a sacrifice bunt, hit a sacrifice fly, or hit behind the runner).

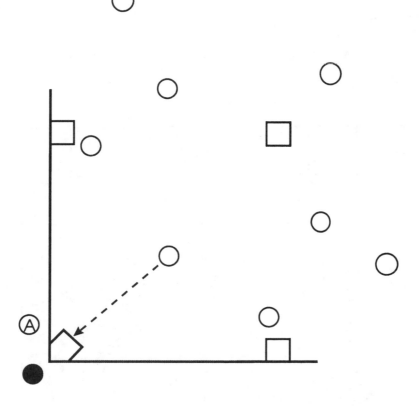

151 COMPETITIVE PLACE HITTING

Objective: To practice the proper mechanics of hitting. To practice fielding. To provide for an inclement weather activity.

Equipment Needed: Bats, rubber or tennis balls, and gloves.

Description: The drill involves dividing the team into four-player groups. The drill can be performed either indoors or outdoors. Each group goes to a separate area of the gymnasium or to a separate area of the playing field which has a fence. Each player on a group has a specific task. One player (A) standing next to a fence or a gymnasium wall serves as a hitter. Another player (B) pitches to A from approximately 50 feet away. The other two players (C and D) closely flank B, one on each side. The drill begins by having player B throw a rubber (or tennis) ball to A. Simultaneously, player C breaks to his right, while D sprints approximately 40 to 50 feet to his left. Using a choke grip, player A is required to tap the ball to C. Player C fields the ball and throws it to D. Player D then returns the ball to B and the drill continues. On the next pitch, everything is the same except that the procedures are reversed: player A must hit the ball to D. After two pitches to player A, the players rotate positions clockwise. The drill involves competition. Points are awarded for performance: two points to a fielder making a clean play and an accurate throw; one point if the batter hits the ball to the correct fielder; no points for any other scenario. The first player earning a preset number of points wins.

Coaching Points:

- The players should constantly switch roles in order to sustain their interest and to give them the opportunity to practice both hitting and fielding.

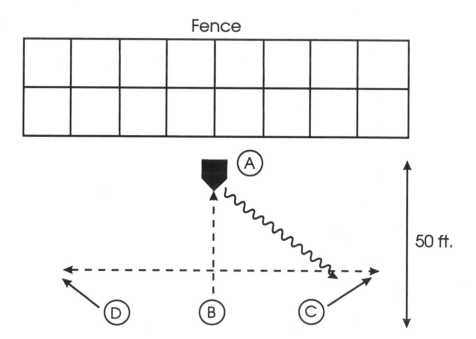

Fence

152 GAME-ACTION WHIFFLE BALL

Objective: To practice the proper mechanics of hitting. To practice hitting under competitive game conditions, and to provide for an inclement weather activity.

Equipment Needed: Bats, gloves, and whiffle balls.

Description: The drill involves players working in pairs: one hitter (A) and one pitcher (B). The drill can be performed both indoors and outdoors. The batter uses his glove as home plate. The pitcher stands approximately 40 feet in front of the hitter and throws (pitches) a whiffle ball which the hitter attempts to hit. Competition is conducted between the two players. A line drive is worth three points. A fly ball over the pitcher's head or a grounder hit past the pitcher is worth two points. An easy pop fly (one hit in front of the pitcher) or an easy ground ball (one fielded by the pitcher) is worth one point. A foul ball or a missed swing receives no points. The hitter is given a preset number of swings before the players switch roles. The player with the most points wins.

Coaching Points:

- The hitter should be encouraged to use proper hitting mechanics.
- This drill can be particularly useful if space is limited.
- The pitchers should be encouraged to mix up their "pitches."
- The competitive aspects can be made even more enjoyable by forming leagues (each player is a one-man team) and keeping standings.

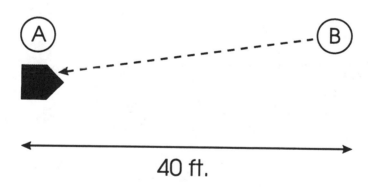

40 ft.

153 RESISTANCE SWINGS

Objective: To develop an increased level of muscular fitness in the muscles involved in hitting.

Equipment Needed: A bat.

Description: The drill involves two players: a hitter and his partner. The hitter assumes his normal batting stance. His partner stands either in front of or behind the hitter and places a very moderate amount of resistance on the bat while the hitter takes a complete swing including the follow-through. If the partner is behind the hitter, he places one hand approximately three to four inches from the bat. The hitter takes a normal swing. The batter catches the bat in his open hand and walks around the hitter to allow him to complete his swing. If the hitter stands in front of the hitter, during the first phase of the drill no resistance is applied. Using a relatively slow speed, the hitter takes a swing while adhering to sound hitting fundamentals. Once the hitter reaches a point where his arms are extended and the bat is out over the plate, his partner places his hand on the bat and lightly resists as the hitter completes his swing.

Coaching Points:

- The resistance provided by the partner should not be so forceful as to cause the hitter to alter any part of his swing, including the follow-through.

154 TIRE SWINGS

Objective: To practice proper hitting mechanics. To develop an increased level of muscular fitness in the muscles involved in hitting.

Equipment Needed: A tire on a rope and a bat.

Description: Working alone, players practice their hitting mechanics by swinging at a tire which is hanging on a rope from a post or other appropriate fixture. The drill involves having a player assume his regular batting stance and then use sound hitting fundamentals while swinging at the tire. The hitter should be required to swing at the tire, make contact with it, drive through it, and complete his follow-through.

Coaching Points:

- Relatively speaking, a tire can provide a reasonable amount of resistance against the swing.
- The drill is virtually without merit if the hitter does not properly follow through on his swing.

6

OFFENSIVE DRILLS

Bunting

155 BUNTING BASICS

Objective: To practice the techniques involved in different types of bunts.

Equipment Needed: Baseballs, a glove, and a bat.

Description: The drill involves two players: a hitter and a tosser. The tosser assumes a kneeling position on one knee, approximately 25 feet in front of the hitter. The tosser throws a ball to the hitter, who practices bunting. After the hitter has practiced hitting a specific type of bunt a preset number of times, the hitter and the tosser trade places. The drill is repeated several times in order to give each player the opportunity to practice a variety of different types of bunts.

Coaching Points:

• As many groups as desired can perform the drill simultaneously.

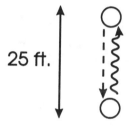

156 BUNTING TECHNIQUES

Objective: To practice the techniques involved in bunting.

Equipment Needed: A screen, baseballs, bats, gloves, and four buckets.

Description: The drill involves dividing the hitters into two groups: with one group at home plate and the other group at second base. A protective screen is in the middle of the pitching area between the two groups. Each group has a designated pitcher and a catcher. The pitcher for group one (A) assumes a position in front of the protective screen and throws to home plate. The pitcher for group two (B), on the other hand, sets up behind the protective screen and throws to second base. Each pitcher has a bucket full of baseballs, while each catcher has an empty bucket next to himself. The drill begins when the first hitter for group one, who is standing at home plate, lays down a specific bunt and runs to first base. At the same time, the first hitter in group two, who is standing at second base, also lays down a preset type of bunt and runs to third base. After bunting, both hitters then jog to the end of the opposite lines.

Coaching Points:

- To make the drill as time-efficient as possible, the baseballs not contacted by the hitter are placed in the empty bucket next to each catcher, thereby allowing the pitcher to prepare for his next pitch.

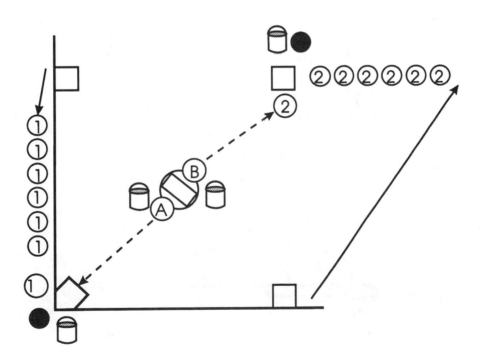

157 BUNTING ACCURATELY

Objective: To practice accurately bunting to a specific area.

Equipment Needed: A rope, baseballs, bats, and two buckets.

Description: A rope is placed 15 feet from home plate in a semicircle from one baseline to another. The pitcher (A) and catcher assume their defensive positions. The pitcher has a bucket full of baseballs, while the catcher has an empty bucket next to himself. All of the hitters line up at home plate. Starting in his regular batting stance, each hitter must bunt the ball and attempt to make it stop inside the rope. The drill begins by having a pitcher throw to home plate. Each hitter gets two opportunities to contact the bunt. If he bunts either the first or second pitch, the hitter must run to first base. On the other hand, if the hitter fails to successfully bunt either ball, he must run around all of the bases before returning to the end of the line.

Coaching Points:

- The pitcher should vary the type, speed, and location of his pitches.
- Variety could be added to the drill by incorporating a first baseman into the drill and requiring the catcher and the pitcher to field the bunts and attempt to throw out the baserunner at first base.

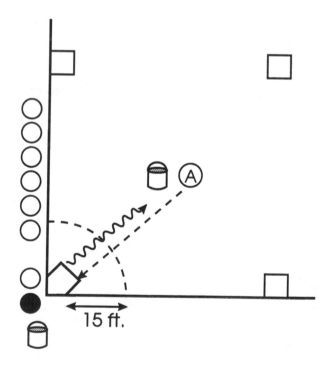

15 ft.

158 SACRIFICE-AND-SLASH WHIFFLE BALL

Objective: To practice the techniques involved in making sacrifice bunts. To practice slash hitting from a stance for sacrifice bunting in a crowded area, without the fear of being hit by a hard thrown ball.

Equipment Needed: A bat, whiffle balls, and gloves.

Description: The drill involves two players: a hitter (A) and a pitcher (B). The batter assumes his regular hitting stance at home plate. The batter sacrifice bunts the first pitch. Then, from a sacrifice bunt hitting stance, he attempts to slash hit the next pitch, a hard ground ball, past an imaginary, drawn-in infielder. After ten repetitions of each type of play, the players then exchange positions. Assuming a stretch position at a distance of approximately 25 to 30 feet, the pitcher uses a whiffle ball to throw fastballs to the hitter.

Coaching Points:

- The drill can involve as many rounds of "sacrifice and slash" drills as the coach deems necessary.
- The drill can be expanded by having the pitcher field both types of balls hit by the batter.

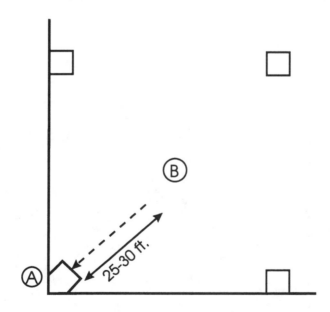

159   CATCH-THE-BALL BUNT

Objective: To teach the bunter to bend his knees while assuming a position to bunt. To develop the ability to not push the bat while bunting.

Equipment Needed: A bat, baseballs, gloves, and a home plate.

Description: The drill involves one player and a coach (or another player). The player places his glove on the end of his bat and assumes his regular batting stance. From the mound, the coach pitches to the hitter who is facing a bunt situation. As the ball leaves the pitcher's hand, the batter pivots into a sacrifice bunt position and kneels down on the ground (right knee on the ground for a right-handed batter, left knee on the ground for a left-handed hitter). The batter then tries to catch the ball with his glove while in the kneeling-bunting position. He quickly learns to cushion the bat toward his body once the ball hits his glove (as opposed to jabbing at the ball).

Coaching Points:

- The batter should keep his hands twelve inches apart on his bat with his lower hand loose and his upper hand firmly next to the knob base in order to hold the bat at eye level.

160 INTRA-SQUAD BUNTING GAME

Objective: To practice the skills and the techniques involved in the "complete" bunting game.

Equipment Needed: A bat, baseballs, gloves, full catching gear, and bases.

Description: The drill involves dividing the team into two squads (A and B) for an intra-squad game. The two teams are only permitted to use the bunting game: drag bunting, sacrifice bunting, hitting behind the runner during a bunt situation, and hitting away from a sacrifice bunting stance. Score is kept. The teams play as many innings of this type of game as the coach chooses.

Coaching Points:

- Despite their importance, the four basic bunting fundamentals often do not receive sufficient attention by many baseball teams. They must be mastered if a team is to play to its fullest potential.

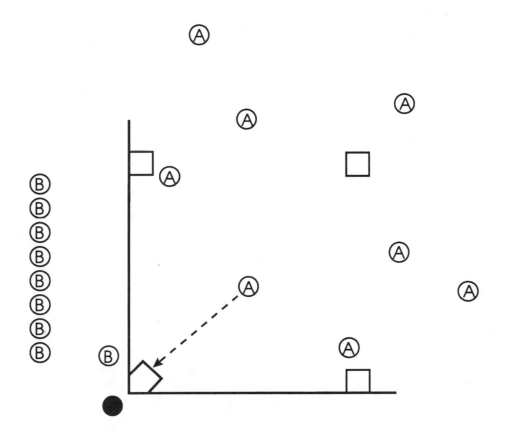

161   THREE-MAN BUNTING GAME

Objective: To practice the techniques involved in making sacrifice and drag bunts. To provide players the maximum amount of bunting practice in the shortest amount of time.

Equipment Needed: Baseballs, a bat, and gloves.

Description: The drill involves three players: one player (A) pitches from a distance of 30 feet, one player hits (B), and the third player (C) shags balls. The players utilize their gloves as boundary markers, one glove serves as a home plate while the other two gloves to mark the third and first base foul lines. The drill begins when the pitcher calls out "sacrifice bunt" and the direction he wants the hitter to bunt the ball, first or third baseline. Throwing with a relatively hard velocity, the pitcher then pitches to the hitter who executes a sacrifice bunt in the designated direction. After the hitter has made ten sacrifice bunts, the players rotate. Once every player has practiced sacrifice bunting, the players go through the drill again, this time while performing drag bunts.

Coaching Points:

- All factors considered, the better the team, the better the ability of its players to bunt. Championships are often won by teams that can best execute the bunting game.
- The players should try to practice bunting as much as time will allow.
- The pitcher must "fire" the ball; if he lobs the ball, the drill will have minimal value.
- Players can create competition by trying to bunt balls into their gloves (somewhat similar to miniature golf).
- The coach can create competition by having three-man teams compete against each other.

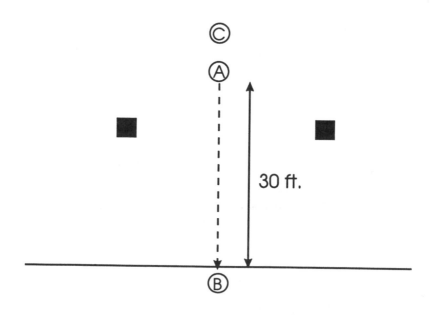

162 FOUR-MAN BUNTING GAME

Objective: To practice the techniques and skills involved in bunting.

Equipment Needed: Baseballs, gloves, bats, and towels.

Description: The drill involves dividing the team's players into groups of four and assigning the groups to positions near the backstop or fence. One player (A) is designated as the hitter. The second player (B) stands approximately 40 feet in front of A and pitches to A. The other two players (C and D) flank B and serve as fielders. Towels are used to designate the baselines. The drill begins when the pitcher, throwing at half speed, delivers a ball to the hitter. The batter attempts to bunt the ball down either baseline. He is given one point if the bunt stays in fair territory. If he pops up, fouls, or misses the pitch, he receives no points. Each hitter keeps track of his points. After a preset number of chances, the athletes rotate positions. The drill requires two rotations (each athlete comes to bat twice). During the second round, the pitcher throws at three-quarter speed. The player earning the most points during the two rounds combined wins.

Coaching Points:

- The hitters should concentrate on watching the ball hit the bat, holding the bat level, and laying the ball on the ground.
- The coach should circulate among the various groups, critique the bunting mechanics of each hitter, and offer help to anyone having difficulty.

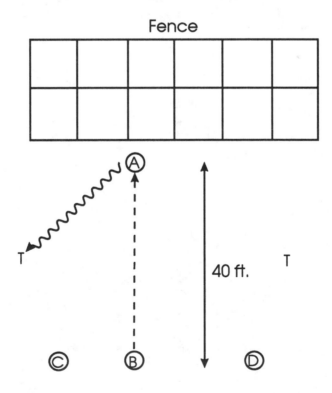

Fence

40 ft.

163 NON-STOP BUNTING

Objective: To practice the techniques and skills involved in sacrifice bunting and drag bunting. To develop and enhance defensive reactions, and to provide the opportunity for a maximum amount of bunting practice in a relatively short period of time.

Equipment Needed: Bats, baseballs, helmets, and gloves.

Description: The drill involves having players work in groups of four. One member of each group serves as the hitter, while the others serve as pitchers and fielders. The batter places his glove on the ground next to him to serve as a home plate. The non-hitters form a line approximately 40 to 45 feet in front of the batter. The drill begins by having the first player in line (A) pitch a ball to the hitter who bunts it. The pitcher then fields the bunt, tosses the ball to the next player in line, and goes to the end of the line. The drill requires that the pitcher must field or retrieve the ball no matter where it goes, even if the hitter fouls the ball back or misses the ball. The next player in line should deliver the next pitch to the hitter as soon as the previous pitcher has fielded the ball and thrown it to him. After the hitter has laid down five sacrifice bunts and five drag bunts, the players rotate positions. The first player in line becomes the new hitter.

Coaching Points:

- The drill should be conducted at a relatively brisk pace in order to maximize the amount of bunt practice and to keep everyone interested.
- The coach should critique the bunting mechanics of the hitter and make corrections as necessary.

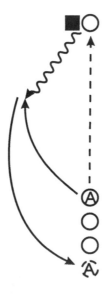

164 SUPER SQUEEZE

Objective: To practice squeeze bunts.

Equipment Needed: Bats, baseballs, and gloves.

Description: The drill involves hitters practicing squeeze bunts in a "live" situation. The pitcher (A), the catcher, the third baseman (C), and the first baseman (B) take their normal positions. A baserunner (D) is placed near third base. The remaining players serve as batters and are given one pitch to bunt. The fielders are required to make plays on all bunted balls; the batter must run out each bunt. The drill begins when the pitcher winds up, the runner leads off from third base, and the batter turns to bunt the pitch. The coach, standing adjacent to the pitcher, then yells out the type of squeeze bunt he wants the hitter to lay down, either a "suicide" or a safety "squeeze." All of the players involved in the drill then react accordingly. Players earn points according to the result of the play. The hitter and the runner are given two points if the runner scores. If the runner is put out, both have a point deducted from their totals. If the batter fouls off or misses the pitch, no points are awarded. After each play, the hitter becomes the runner, while the runner goes to the end of the line of batters. The player earning the most points wins.

Coaching Points:

- If a pitcher sees that a runner is leaving too early from third base, he should throw the batter a particularly tough pitch to bunt, such as, high and outside for left-handed hitters or high and inside for right-handed hitters.
- The coach should periodically rotate new players into the field.
- The two main types of squeeze bunts, suicide and delayed, usually require countless hours of practice to master.

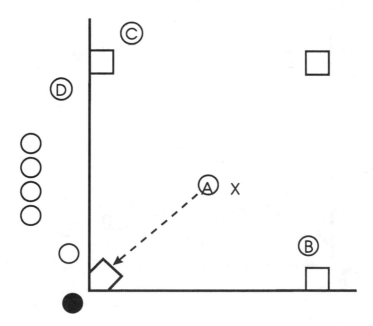

165 BUNT AND RUN SPRINTS

Objective: To practice bunting techniques and skills. To practice fielding bunts, and to develop stamina.

Equipment Needed: Bats, baseballs, gloves, bases, and four cones.

Description: The drill involves having the pitcher (A), the catcher, the third baseman (E), the shortstop (D), second baseman (C), and the first baseman (B) assume their positions in the field. Two-foot wide "safe zones" are marked off down each baseline with the cones: one zone per baseline. Those players not in the field or not participating in another drill at the same time line up and act as hitters. The drill begins by having the pitcher throw at approximately three-quarter speed to the first hitter in line. The hitter attempts to bunt the ball fairly and beat the throw to first base. The players in the field pick up the bunt and attempt to throw out the hitter at first. The hitters alternate after each ball bunted fairly. Points are awarded according to the outcome of the play. The offense (the hitters) are given one point for each bunt they beat out, plus an additional point for any bunt hit on the ground between the cones (the "safe zones") whether the batter gets thrown out or not. The defense (the fielders) are given one point for each runner they throw out. The first group to score five points wins. The "losing" squad must run five mad-dog, home-to-first-and-back sprints. (Note: Each round-trip counts as one sprint.)

Coaching Points:

- The coach should periodically change the players in the field.
- Hitters should work on bat control while bunting.

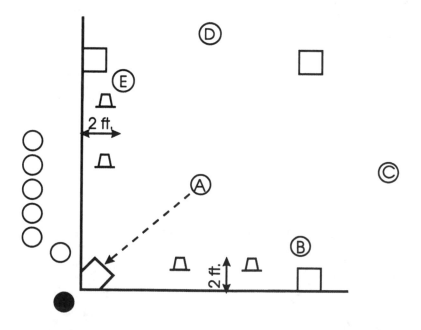

166 GAME-ACTION BUNTING

Objective: To practice bunting and fielding techniques and skills. To provide an inclement weather activity.

Equipment Needed: Bats, gloves, tennis (or rubber) balls, and bases.

Description: This drill can be performed outdoors or indoors. Outdoors, it is performed on a regulation diamond. Indoors, a diamond is set up with moveable rubber bases. The drill involves teams of infielders with six players per team. Play begins when one complete team of infielders takes the field. The catcher wears full protective equipment. The other team is on offense. One player on the offensive team is assigned as a baserunner to first base. The other offensive players line up. The first player in line then comes to the plate as a batter. The primary goal of the offense is to score runs; it's the hitter's job to advance the runner. The batter receives two pitches per time at bat; he must bunt one of the pitches. Every offensive player bats twice each inning. If the batter fails to bunt the ball into fair territory, he's out. He then returns to the end of the line. Against a six-man team, the pitcher must pitch (using a tennis or a rubber ball) to 12 batters each inning. If the pitcher fails to throw a strike or hits the batter, the batter is awarded first base, forcing any existing baserunners to move up a base. The next man in line then comes to the plate. After every three outs, any runners on base leave the base and return to the end of the line. Another player goes to first base and play continues. After every hitter bats twice, the sides change regardless of the number of outs: the offensive and defensive teams switch roles. Runners advance on walks, tag-ups, wild pitches, passed balls, errors, and bunts. Runners are not permitted to slide or interfere with play. The catcher (or a coach) empires the game. The game lasts five innings. The team scoring the most runs wins. Players on the losing team can be required to perform calisthenics on run sprints.

Coaching Points:

- Using prearranged signals, the offensive team can practice specific game-situation plays (suicide or safety squeeze, run and bunt, and fake bunt and run plays, for example).
- The defenders should concentrate on adhering to proper fielding mechanics.
- The coach should critique all plays and make corrections as necessary.

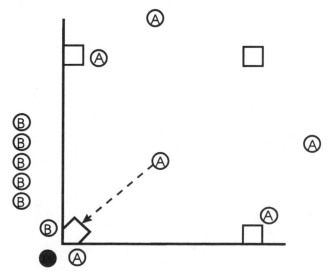

7

OFFENSIVE DRILLS

Baserunning

167 OUT OF THE BOX QUICKLY

Objective: To practice breaking out of the batter's box quickly and explosively.

Equipment Needed: Four bats and four bases.

Description: The drill involves four players who form a square, approximately 45 feet apart. A base is placed on each corner of the square. The batters assume their regular hitting stance (with a bat). On a command from the coach, all of the players swing at a "phantom pitch," break out of the hypothetical batter's box, and sprint to their right to the next base. Each group of players should go around the square at least seven times: three times swinging away, twice drag bunting, and then twice sacrifice bunting.

Coaching Points:

- The coach should point out the similarity of the drill to having track athletes practice their starts from starting blocks.
- Several "box stations" can be set up so that a maximum number of players can be working at the same time.
- The distance between the bases is shortened in order to emphasize the techniques involved in breaking out of the batter's box.

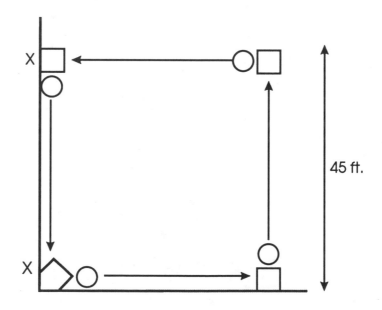

45 ft.

168 SPRINT PAST FIRST

Objective: To teach players to always overrun first base; to develop stamina.

Equipment Needed: Three first bases and three home plates.

Description: Three home plates and three first bases are set up at regulation distance. The players form three lines, with one line standing at each home plate. The first player in each line assumes his regular batting stance. The drill begins by having the hitter (who is standing in the hypothetical batter's box) simulate a swing and then sprint to and past first base. Each time a player touches first base, he should turn his head to the right in order to develop the habit of checking for overthrows by infielders during a real game situation. Depending upon the situation, this step may help the runner to advance to second base. Once he has run past first base, each player jogs back to the end of his line, avoiding any other baserunner who is involved in the drill. As the drill progresses, the players should be required to run harder.

Coaching Points:

- Variety could be added to the drill by incorporating timed competition between the three lines. For example, each line of players could compete as a relay team against the other lines. The next player in each line starts as soon as the preceding player steps on first base. The first team (line) done wins the relay.

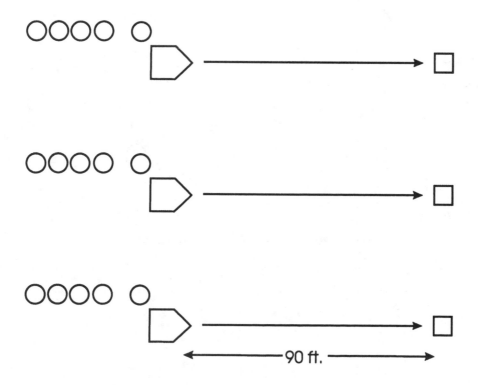

169 LEAD-OFF AND PICK-OFF DRILL

Objective: To practice proper baserunning fundamentals; to practice pick-off techniques.

Equipment Needed: A base (a glove can be used) and a ball (optional).

Description: The drill involves two players, a pitcher (A) and a baserunner (B), who position themselves anywhere in the outfield or off the field. A base (or the player's glove) is placed on the ground next to the baserunner. The baserunner practices all types of leads demanded by various game situations at all the bases. At the same time, the pitcher works on simulating his pick-off motion to the base where the runner is standing or his motion to the plate. The runner should concentrate on the fundamental factors involved in effective baserunning (quickness, timing, alertness, aggressiveness, and precision).

Coaching Points:

- The baserunner and the pitcher should visualize that they are in an actual game situation and react to each other's movements accordingly.

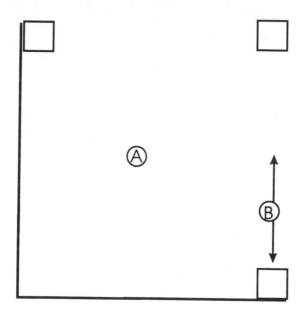

170 LEAD-OFF REACTION DRILL

Objective: To practice the proper techniques involved in both assuming leads and baserunning from each base and to practice pick-off moves.

Equipment Needed: Gloves (for pitchers).

Description: The drill involves having three pitchers form a small circle around the pitcher's mound and face home plate. The non-pitchers (B) form into three lines of equal size. One line of players stands at each base. The drill begins by having the pitchers simulate pitching from the stretch position and either deliver an imaginary pitch to the plate or execute a pick-off move to the base closest to them. After five simulated pitches, the pitchers rotate around the "circle" one space so that each pitcher gets to practice his pick-off moves to each of the three bases. While the pitchers are simulating their moves, the runners practice taking a lead-off and breaking for the next base from the base where they are stationed. The key is to have the baserunner concentrate on the pitcher and react accordingly.

Coaching Points:

- The drill should last approximately 10 to 12 minutes.
- Baserunners should rotate to the next base when the pitchers rotate positions.
- The drill can be expanded by having the next player in each line act as an infielder and receive a pitcher's attempted pick-off throw.

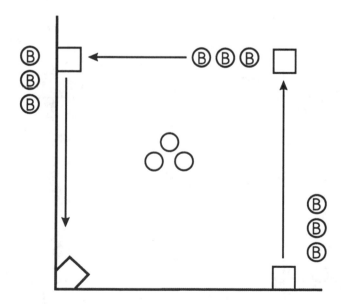

171 SPRINT AROUND THE BASES

Objective: To develop the ability to leave bases and the batter's box quickly. To practice baserunning skills and techniques (stopping, rounding, or running through appropriate bases) and to develop stamina.

Equipment Needed: Three bases and a home plate.

Description: The drill involves dividing the team into four groups of approximately the same size. One group is assigned to each base, including home plate. The first player in each group participates in the drill as a baserunner at the base adjacent to his group. The first player in the home plate group starts in the batter's box. The diamond should be set up as usual: preferably in the outfield where running and sliding would be less likely to result in an injury. On the coach's command, "Go," each of the four players sprints to the next base. The two players running toward second base and third base must stop, while the two beginning the drill at home and third base must run through first base and home plate respectively. After a preset number of plays, the players rotate. The baserunners go to the end of their lines, while the next player in line becomes the new baserunner.

Coaching Points:

- The coach should specify the type of lead off he wants the runners on first, second, and third base to take.
- The drill can be varied by requiring the baserunners (except for the one running from home to first) to execute different types of slides.

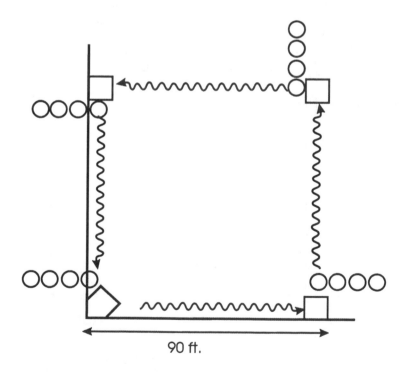

90 ft.

172 CATCH ME IF YOU CAN

Objective: To practice basic baserunning techniques and develop stamina.

Equipment Needed: A baseball diamond and bases.

Description: The drill involves dividing the team into two groups of equal size (A and B) and approximately equal speed. One group begins the drill at home plate, while the other group starts at second base. On the coach's signal, the first person in each line runs all the bases and then tags the next runner in his line, who also runs all the bases. The drill continues until one team catches up to the other team. The focus of the drill is to have the baserunner of one team try to catch and tag the other team's runner. The losing team can be required to perform sprints or push-ups.

Coaching Points:

- The coach should make sure that each runner touches every base and tags the next player in his line.
- The drill can be varied by dividing the team into four groups. As one group catches another, the group which has been "tagged" sits out of the drill until only one group remains untagged (the winner).

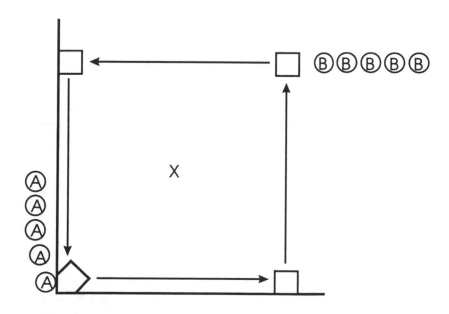

173 CHASE 'EM, CATCH 'EM

Objective: To improve foot speed. To develop the ability to move quickly and explosively.

Equipment Needed: A baseball diamond.

Description: The drill involves having the players divide into two groups and line up at first base and third base respectively. The first two players in each line participate in the drill. The first player (A and B) in each line assumes a position approximately 10 feet from first base and third base respectively. On the command of the coach assigned to a particular line, the next player in line (C and D) attempts to catch the baserunner from his line before that player can reach second base and home plate respectively. If the baserunner reaches base successfully, he continues as the baserunner; if not, he goes to the end of the line and the players move up.

Coaching Points:

- The drill can be conducted on a competitive basis. Each baserunner who gets to the next base without being tagged is awarded one point. The first player to earn five points wins the contest.
- Variety can be added to the drill by having the baserunner slide into the next base when he gets there.

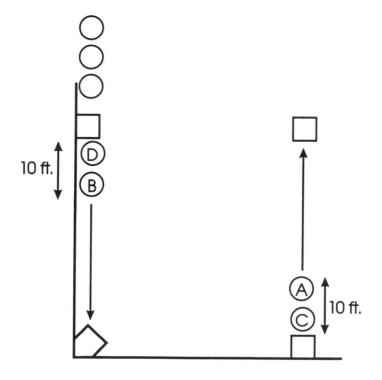

174 BOX RUNNING - SUPER BREAK

Objective: To practice breaking toward the next base.

Equipment Needed: Four bases.

Description: The drill involves five players: four positional players and a pitcher. A "box" is set up by placing four bases in a square, 45 feet from each other. The drill begins by having the pitcher assume a position in the middle of the box and placing one positional player at each base. Each positional player takes a 10 foot leadoff, while watching the pitcher closely. From the stretch position, the pitcher feigns a pitch to home. At that point, the runners then all break to the next base, concentrating on ensuring that their take-off is both quick and explosive.

Coaching Points:

- The coach should set up boxes so that all positional players can practice this drill at the same time.
- The coach can decide whether a jab step or a crossover step is used to initiate the break.
- This drill provides the opportunity to practice 16 to 20 breaks in only a few minutes' time.

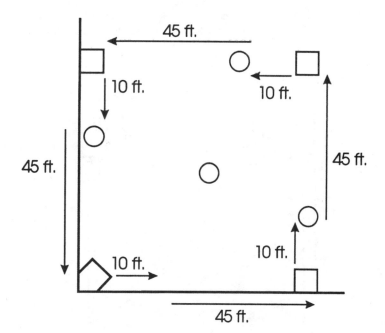

175 BOX RUNNING - SPRINT AND SLIDE

Objective: To practice properly rounding a base, tagging the inside of the base, continuing to the next base, and sliding. To develop stamina.

Equipment Needed: Four bases.

Description: The team divides into two groups. The drill involves three players: two positional players (the first player in each line [A and B]) and a pitcher. A "box" is set up by placing four bases in a square, 60 feet from each other. The drill begins by having the pitcher assume a position in the middle of the box and placing the two positional players on opposite bases, diagonally to each other. Each positional player visualizes that he is a batter who, after swinging at a hypothetical pitch, must run out a double. The drill begins by having the pitcher feign throwing a pitch. Each of the positional players swings at the phantom ball and runs to what would be second base in a live situation. When he gets to second base, he slides away from a phantom tag put on him by the next player in the line at that base. After the play, the players rotate positions.

Coaching Points:

- Each player should concentrate on rounding first base, tagging it on the inside corner and going directly towards second base, before making a good slide into second.
- The shorter distances between bases (60 feet) gives players an opportunity to perform more repetitions of the drill without undue fatigue setting in.
- Variety can be added to the drill by having the batter run their "hits" into either triples or inside-the-park home runs, in addition to doubles.

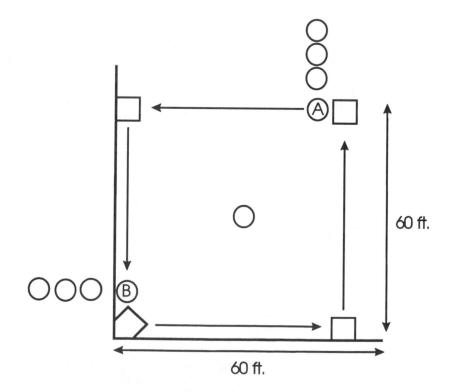

176 STOPWATCH BASERUNNING

Objective: To practice baserunning mechanics. To improve foot speed.

Equipment Needed: Stopwatches, bases, whiffle balls, and bats.

Description: The drill involves dividing the team into four groups and assigning each group to a station. A station consists of two bases which are ninety feet apart. The first player in line takes his regular batting position next to the base (hypothetically, home plate). The next player in line, using the flip drill, flips a whiffle ball at the hitter. The batter hits the whiffle ball and sprints to first base. A coach or another player times how long it takes the batter to reach first base. Runners are required to emphasize good running mechanics to break the tape at first base, to nod the bag with their head, so they don't miss it, to brake down after tagging the base, and to look into foul territory to see if the throw got past the first baseman.

Coaching Points:

- All factors considered, when baserunners are timed, they tend to get faster.
- Competition can be conducted in the drill by timing each player a preset number of times and acknowledging the fastest player at each position.
- The drill can be modified to work on having baserunners practice leading off and stealing, either first to second or second to third. In this instance, players take a 10 to 12 foot lead and use a head-first slide, eight to ten feet away, into the next base.

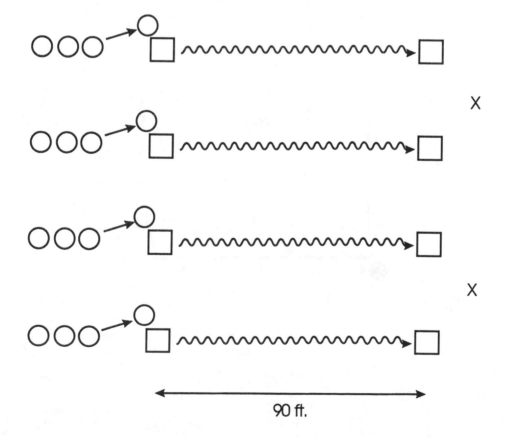

90 ft.

177 BALL IN DIRT - RUNNERS BREAK

Objective: To teach baserunners to read and react to the actions of the catcher on wild pitches.

Equipment Needed: Full catching gear, baseballs, and gloves.

Description: The drill involves six participants at a time: a pitcher (A), a catcher, two position fielders (a third baseman [B]and a shortstop[C]), and two baserunners (one at first base [D]and one at second base[E]). The drill begins by having the baserunners take a normal lead off base. The pitcher throws a low pitch to the catcher who blocks the ball with his chest. The baserunners read and react to the blocked ball. They then break for the next base and slide into the base. The catcher should scramble after the ball and go through the mechanics of attempting to throw out one of the runners. After the play, the players rotate positions.

Coaching Points:

- Early in the season, the distance between the bases can be shortened to lessen the strain on the catcher's arm.

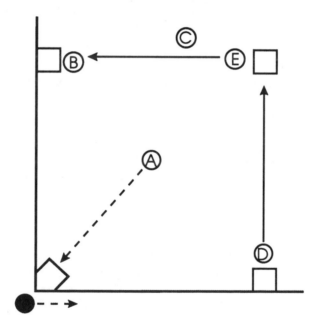

178 HIT AND RUN, RUN, RUN

Objective: To practice having the baserunner on first break for second on the hit and run play and to be able to see the ball being hit directly at him, to jump over the ball, and to race to third base on the play.

Equipment Needed: Several tennis balls or whiffle balls.

Description: The team divides into two groups. One group lines up adjacent to first base, while the other group is positioned next to third base. The first player in each line (A and B) serves as a baserunner and takes a normal lead. The next player in each line (C) acts as a simulated hitter and lines up facing the baserunner approximately 15 to 20 feet from him. The drill is conducted on a regular baseball diamond, but both baserunners simulate breaking from first base and taking third on the hit and run. As the baserunners break, the two "hitters" roll hard ground balls at them trying to hit the runners. The runners avoid getting hit and race to third base.

Coaching Points:

- Tennis balls or whiffle balls are used by the "hitters" so that the baserunners aren't injured by the ball if they get hit by it.

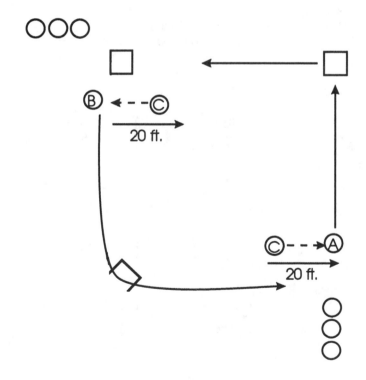

179 RUNDOWN

Objective: To practice having baserunners get out of, or break up, a rundown.

Equipment Needed: Tennis balls or rubber balls.

Description: The entire team divides into two groups, each of which works on getting out of a rundown. One group consists of the infielders and half of the outfielders. The other group has the rest of the outfielders along with the pitchers and the catchers. Three players from each group work on the rundown play at a time: one serves as a baserunner (A), while the other two act as positional fielders (B and C). The key for the baserunner is to break hard towards a base, trying to force an early throw by the defensive player with the ball. When the early throw is made, the runner applies the brakes and turns around, running full speed in the other direction at the player waiting for the return throw. While running, the baserunner tries to line himself up with the defensive player who is receiving the throw and tries to get hit in the back with the ball when (and if) it is thrown. If the baserunner can run into the fielder while going back to a base, interference will be called on the defense. After each play, the players all rotate positions.

Coaching Points:

- The drill can be expanded by adding another player to act as a pitcher. The pitcher in this instance would initiate the drill by throwing to the "first baseman." The baserunner would allow himself to be picked off, thereby setting up the rundown play.
- The drill should emphasize adhering to the proper mechanics of the rundown play by the positional players, as well as the baserunners.

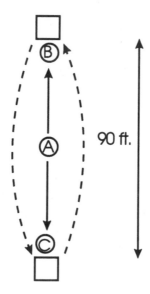

180 BOX DRILL - TAGGING UP

Objective: To practice having baserunners tag up on fly balls and break to the next base as a fly ball is being caught by an outfielder.

Equipment Needed: Four bases, a baseball, and a glove.

Description: Four bases are set up in a square (box), approximately 45 feet apart. The coach stands in the center of the box. A baserunner is assigned to each base. Each baserunner takes a normal lead. The drill begins by having the coach throw a pop-up to himself, high enough for the baserunners to retreat to the base, tag up, and break to the next base after the coach has caught the ball. After a preset number of tag-up plays (for example, twice caught around the box), the players rotate positions.

Coaching Points:

- Several box stations can be set up to maximize the number of players actively involved in the drill at one time.
- After the players have mastered the basic techniques involved in tagging up, the distance between the bases can gradually be lengthened to ninety feet to incorporate more conditioning aspects into the drill.

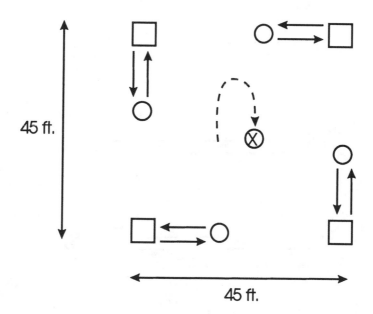

181 RUNNING TO THE SIGNS

Objective: To review and reinforce the players' knowledge and reactions to offensive signs. To develop stamina.

Equipment Needed: None.

Description: The drill involves dividing the team into two groups. Each group has a coach assigned to it. The coach gives offensive signs to the players in that group. The two groups line up approximately 60 feet apart from each other. The drill begins by having one group of players get a sign from a coach. After giving the sign, the coach then acts as a pitcher feigning a pitch to home plate. The runners break according to the sign given to them by the coach and sprint 60 feet to the other area where the other group is located. Simultaneously, the coach goes through the same routine at the other end and the runners go back and forth about 12 times.

Coaching Points

- Coaches can give a variety of signs (for example, steal of home sign, running on the lefties sign, first and third signs, or walking leads). One of the major benefits of the drill is that the constant review leaves very little chance of a player missing a sign in the game.
- During every practice and prior to every game, the players should review the offensive signs while running sprints in the outfield.

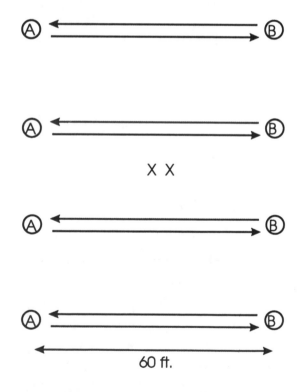

182 MIRROR - REACTION

Objective: To improve reaction time and develop stamina. To practice the proper footwork.

Equipment Needed: Bases

Description: The drill involves players working in pairs. Each pair assumes a position adjacent to a base. One player (A) takes his normal lead off from base, while the second player (B) stands four to five feet behind him (also in the base path). The focus of the drill is to have player B mirror the actions of A who is in front of him. Whatever way player A breaks, B tries to beat him to his destination, either to the next base or back to the base. As a general rule, a team should run 15 to 20 90-foot mirrors after a game to condition the squad and work on improving player quickness.

Coaching Points:

- This is an excellent drill to improve both reaction time and overall conditioning.
- The coach should emphasize using proper footwork to take and initial, explosive step.

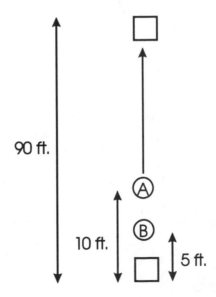

8

OFFENSIVE DRILLS

Sliding

183 HANDS UP, SAFE SLIDING

Objective: To teach the skills and techniques of sliding in an environment which minimizes the possibility of a player's being injured.

Equipment Needed: Bases (or gloves) and bats.

Description: The drill involves one or more players working alone while practicing sliding techniques. The drill is conducted on a progressive basis: from the simple to the complex. During the drill, players should be required to wear long pants or sliding pads. Initially, each player should practice "walking through" the steps involved in sliding several times before trying it at full speed. During the initial stages of the drill, players walk through the fundamentals of the stand-up slide while holding a bat over their heads in order to practice keeping their hands off the ground during the slide. A player's right knee should be bent upward and his right heel should be off the ground as he lands softly on his rear. Once a player is able to master the "feel" of the specific fundamentals of sliding, he should execute stand-up slides into a base or into a glove placed on the ground to serve as a base. A player begins to develop the proper rhythm and timing of executing slides at full speed, he should practice the techniques of sliding to either side of the base and touching the base with his hand.

Coaching Points:

- In the later stages of the drill, players should practice sliding into a base, immediately getting up and advancing to the next base, or decoy sliding around a base to avoid a tag.
- Among the advantages of the stand-up slide is the fact that it permits players to slide away from tags by using the decoy slide, or to be able to quickly advance to the next base on an overthrow.

184 BOX DRILL - SLIDING

Objective: To teach and practice the techniques of sliding in a relatively condensed area. To provide an indoor activity during inclement weather.

Equipment Needed: Bases and gloves.

Description: The drill involves dividing the team into four groups. Each group is assigned to one of four bases which are placed in a square formation approximately 45 feet apart. The first player in each line participates in the drill as a baserunner. The coach (or another player) stands in the middle of the box and serves as a simulated pitcher. The drill begins by having the "pitcher" feign a throw to home. Each of the four baserunners having taken a normal lead then breaks for the next base, sprints to the base, and performs the type of slide called for by the coach (for example, the fade-away slide, the stand-up slide, or sliding head first).

Coaching Points:

- This drill can be performed either outdoors or indoors.
- If drill is being conducted outdoors, it should be performed in the outfield. The players should take off their spiked shoes and use their gloves as bases.
- If the drill is held indoors, the coach should require that the players wear both sweat pants and long-sleeved jerseys (to cover their elbows) to protect the players against floor burns.

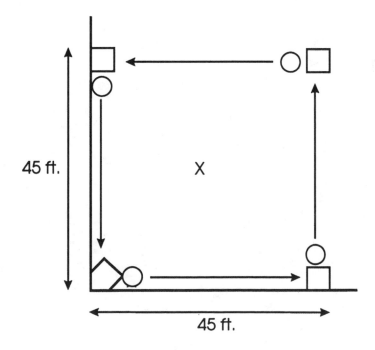

185   BEAR CRAWL AND SLIDE

Objective: To teach baserunners to get over their fear of injuring themselves while sliding.

Equipment Needed: Gloves.

Description: The drill is performed on the outfield grass. The drill involves having the players form one line facing the coach who is standing approximately 40 feet away. The players then place or throw their gloves approximately 25 feet in front of them. Each glove serves as a base as a contact point for sliding. The drill begins by having the players get in a bear crawl position (hands and feet on the ground). On command from the coach, the players bear crawl as quickly as they can to their own glove and practice sliding into the "base." Sliding from an all-fours position helps cushion the player's fall (momentum) and takes away some of the pain when his thigh hits the ground.

Coaching Points:

- This drill provides the means for players to work on three types of slides: the stand-up slide, the fade-away slide, and the head first slide.

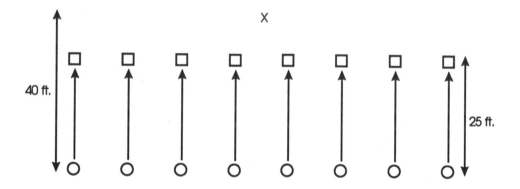

186 GROUP SLIDING

Objective: To teach and practice the techniques of having a baserunner tuck one leg while performing a bent-leg slide.

Equipment Needed: None.

Description: The drill involves having the team spread out and form up on the outfield grass facing the coach. Each player sits on the ground with his arms extended behind him to support his upper body. His legs are extended in front of him towards the coach with the knees slightly bent. On command from the coach, each player raises his body to an inverted low crawl position (he supports himself on his hands and feet). Each player then falls slightly backwards to the ground. Simultaneously, he tucks one leg underneath himself in a "4" shape. At the same time, he throws his arms in front of his body while keeping his hands up in the air.

Coaching Points:

- The coach should walk among his players while they are performing the drill and critique them as needed.

187 READ AND SLIDE

Objective: To practice the techniques of both bent-leg and head-first sliding. To practice reading the signs of the first base coach. To improve reaction time.

Equipment Needed: Baseballs and bases.

Description: The drill involves having all of the players line up at home plate. The coach stands on the edge of the outfield grass in left field with several baseballs. The assistant coach assumes a position in the coach's box at first base. The drill begins by having the first player in line serve as a batter/baserunner. On command from the coach, the batter sprints to first base, where he is given a signal by the assistant coach to turn and check to see if he should attempt to advance to second base. As he rounds first base, the baserunner should locate the coach who is standing in left field. The coach is holding a baseball. If he drops the ball, the baserunner should continue on to second and perform a bent-leg slide. On the other hand, if the coach brings the ball back to his body and acts as if he is going to throw the ball to first base, the baserunner should go back to first base as quickly as possible and perform a head-first slide into first.

Coaching Points:

- The coach should critique the baserunner's slide into second base, while the assistant coach should assess the runner's technique for performing the head-first slide into first base.

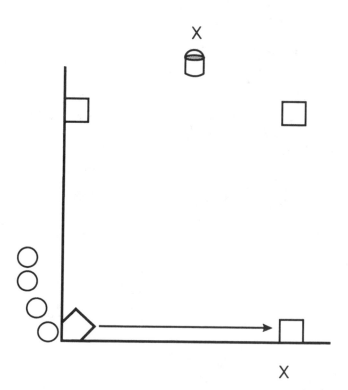

9

SPECIAL CATEGORY DRILLS

Pick-Off Plays

188 PICK-OFF — BASIC RUNDOWN

Objective: To teach the first baseman to make a quick accurate throw to second base after the pitcher has picked-off the baserunner at first base and the baserunner has broken for second base. To have infielders practice the rundown play.

Equipment Needed: Gloves, bases, and baseballs.

Description: The drill involves four players: a pitcher (A), a first baseman (B), a middle infielder (C), and a baserunner at first base (D). The drill begins by having the pitcher make a throw to the first baseman to pick-off the baserunner. The first baseman then fires the ball to the middle infielder in an attempt to get the baserunner who was picked-off. He then follows his throw in case there is an ensuing rundown. He and the middle infielder execute the rundown play. The baserunner attempts to avoid the tag and get either back to first or down to second. After a preset number of plays, the players switch positions.

Coaching Points:

- The coach should emphasize to the first baseman that the baserunner should be tagged out as quickly as possible.
- The coach can incorporate competition into the drill by having the two fielders run sprints or perform push-ups every time the baserunner is able to get back to the base safely.

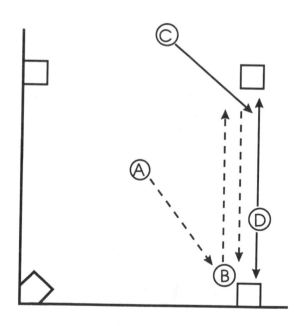

189 PICK-OFF — BUNT PLAY RUNDOWN

Objective: To practice the techniques involved in pick-off and rundown plays in a bunting situation.

Equipment Needed: Gloves, bases, and baseballs.

Description: The drill involves practicing pick-off and rundown plays in a bunting situation. The team is divided into two groups: position players in the field (A) and baserunners (B). The players in the field assume their regular defensive positions in a bunting situation: the pitcher, the catcher, the first baseman, the second baseman, the third baseman, and the shortstop. The baserunners line up at first base, with the first player in line serving as the baserunner. The drill begins by having the pitcher throw a pitch to the catcher. At the same time, the baserunner at first base takes an aggressive lead, while the second baseman simultaneously breaks hard to cover first base. The catcher then makes a pick-off throw to the second baseman at first base to catch the runner in a rundown situation. At that point, the second baseman runs at the baserunner to make him commit to running toward second base. Once the baserunner has run about halfway to second, the second baseman then throws the ball to the shortstop, who is between the baserunner and second and who is moving toward the runner. The shortstop completes the rundown play by chasing the baserunner back towards first base and either tagging the baserunner out or tossing the ball to the first baseman (who has returned to first base) so that he can make the tag play.

Coaching Points:

- The drill can be expanded by adding more baserunners and creating different types of situations.

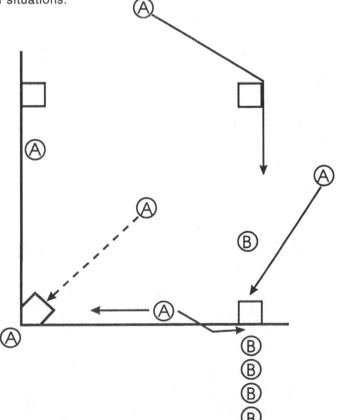

190 PICK-OFF — CATCHER TO FIRST OR THIRD

Objective: To have catchers practice the pick-off play throw to either first base or third.

Equipment Needed: Full catcher's gear, bases, baseballs, and gloves.

Description: The drill involves having the catcher practice pick-off throws to either first base or third base in a bunting situation. The team is divided into two groups: position players (A) (pitcher, catcher, first baseman, second baseman, third baseman, and shortstop, all of whom are at their defensive positions) and base-runners (B) (who are lined up at either first base or third base). The drill begins by having the pitcher throw a pitch to the catcher. On the release of the pitch, both baserunners take an aggressive lead. Simultaneously, when the pitcher releases the ball, the second baseman quickly moves to cover first base, while the short-stop quickly goes over to cover third base. The catcher then makes a pick-off throw to either first base or third base.

Coaching Points:

- The coach should require that the catcher wear full protective catching gear during the drill.
- On a specific pick-off play to either first base or third base during a bunting situation, both the first baseman and the third baseman should break toward home plate when the pitch is released in order to distract the runner's attention and give the second baseman or the shortstop the opportunity to come in from behind without being detected.

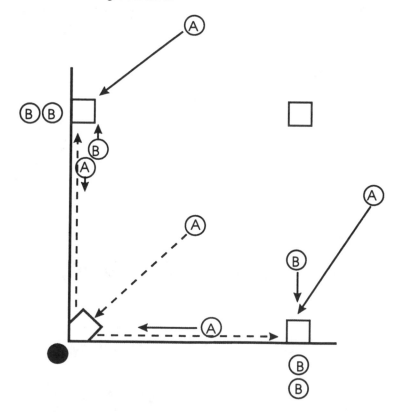

10

SPECIAL CATEGORY DRILLS

Bunt Defense

191 BUNT DEFENSE - TWO MAN

Objective: To teach catchers to field bunts correctly and make a quick, accurate throw to the bases.

Equipment Needed: Full catcher's gear, baseballs, and gloves.

Description: The drill involves catchers working in pairs. One catcher (A) rolls his own bunt to various locations in front of himself, pounces on the ball, and throws to the other catcher (B) who is approximately 60 to 80 feet away. Player A can set up any hypothetical situation he wants. He can throw to first or second base, or position himself in such a way that he can be working for a force-out at third base. After player A throws to B, they exchange roles. Each catcher should make approximately a dozen throws to first base and six throws each to both second base and third base.

Coaching Points:

- The coach should emphasize that the catcher should use his glove in scooping the ball into his throwing hand. The catcher should not attempt to bare hand the ball unless it's the only play he has.

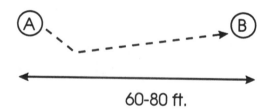

60-80 ft.

192 DRAG BUNT DEFENSE

Objective: To teach the first baseman and the pitcher the techniques involved in fielding a drag bunt.

Equipment Needed: A base, gloves, and baseballs.

Description: The drill involves three players: a pitcher (A), a first baseman (B), and another player who serves as a feeder. The pitcher and the first baseman line up in their "normal" positions. The feeder sets up adjacent to home plate. The drill begins by having the feeder roll the ball in the area between the pitcher and the first baseman, simulating a drag bunt. The pitcher and the first baseman make an instant judgment that the pitcher may not be able to handle the bunt. As a result, the pitcher realizes that the first baseman must race in and attempt to field the ball. At the same time, the pitcher continues trying to field the bunt. If he does field the ball, he scoops it up and races to beat the baserunner (the feeder) to the bag. If the pitcher can't reach the ball, the first baseman must field it and shovel it to him. In the latter instance, the pitcher takes the toss from the first baseman, continues on to first base, and tags the bag.

Coaching Points:

- In either instance, the pitcher should make the play at first because his momentum is already in that direction. On the other hand, because the first baseman is charging in toward the plate to make the play, he would have to brake himself and change directions.

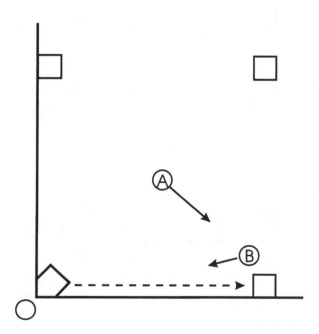

193 BUNT DEFENSE - FIRST BASEMAN

Objective: To have first basemen field bunts and practice throwing out runners at all the bases, including home.

Equipment Needed: A base, baseballs, and gloves.

Description: The drill involves two first basemen and a position fielder. One first baseman (A) acts as a batter. The drill begins by having player A standing approximately 90 feet away (at home plate) roll a bunt toward the other first baseman (B). Player B breaks in and fields the ball, wheels and throws to the fielder (C), who is positioned at a predesignated base. Player B should make five throws to each base, including home plate (to simulate making the squeeze play), and then exchange places with A.

Coaching Points:

- The drill can be expanded by adding one or more baserunners.
- The player acting as the batter (A) should vary the location and the speed of the simulated bunts he rolls to the first baseman (B).

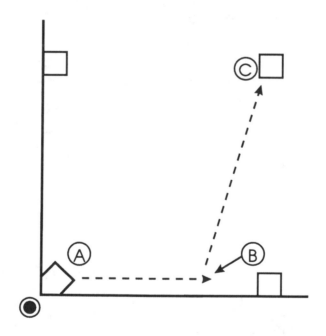

194 BUNT DEFENSE - BASERUNNER AT FIRST BASE

Objective: To have infielders practice defending against a bunt when a baserunner is on first base. To practice baserunning and sliding techniques.

Equipment Needed: A bat, baseballs, and gloves.

Description: The drill involves having a full set of infielders, including the pitcher, at their regular defensive positions. The rest of the team divides into two groups. One group acts as hitters (A), while the other group serves as baserunners (B). The first player in the hitter's line is at bat and the first man in the baserunner's line is on first base. The drill requires that the fielders must defend against four possible bunt situation scenarios. Each scenario begins by having the pitcher throw to the hitter who must bunt the ball (anywhere he chooses) and then attempt to beat out the bunt. In the first scenario, the defense fields the bunt and throws the ball to first base which is covered by the second baseman. The second baseman checks the baserunner who has advanced to second base to see if he has rounded the base too far. In the second scenario, the defense fields the bunt and again throws the ball to first base to the second baseman. In this situation, the second baseman quickly fires the ball to second base in an attempt to get the baserunner, who has rounded the base too far. In the third scenario, the defense fields the bunt, but this time throws the ball to second base to the shortstop who is covering the base in an attempt to turn the double play. In the fourth scenario, the defense fields the bunt and throws the ball to first base to the second baseman. The second baseman then fires the ball to third base in an attempt to get the baserunner, who is attempting to advance to third base from first base on the play.

Coaching Points:

- The coach and his assistants should critique each player's performance to ensure his adherence to proper techniques.

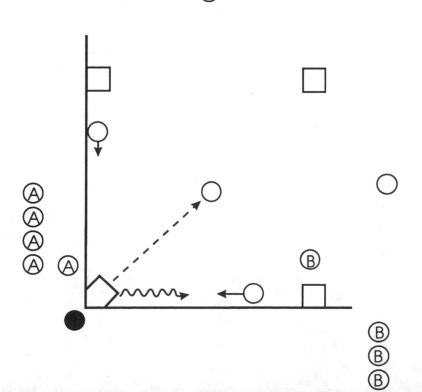

195 BUNT DEFENSE - BASERUNNER AT SECOND BASE

Objective: To have infielders practice defending against a bunt when a baserunner is on second base. To practice baserunning and sliding techniques.

Equipment Needed: A bat, baseballs, and gloves.

Description: The drill involves having a full set of infielders, including the pitcher, at their regular defensive positions. The rest of the team divides into two groups. One group acts as hitters (A), while the other group serves as baserunners (B). The first player in the hitter's line is at bat while the first man in the baserunner's line is on second base. The drill requires that the fielders must defend against two possible bunt situation scenarios. Each scenario begins by having the pitcher throw to the hitter who must bunt the ball (anywhere he chooses) and then attempt to beat out the bunt. In the first scenario, the defense fields the bunt and checks the baserunner who is advancing to third base from second base. After determining that the baserunner cannot be thrown out at third base, the defense then throws the ball to first base to get the hitter. In the second scenario, the defense fields the bunt, but this time throws the ball to third base in an attempt to tag the baserunner out.

Coaching Points:

• The coach and his assistants should critique each player's performance to ensure his adherence to proper techniques.

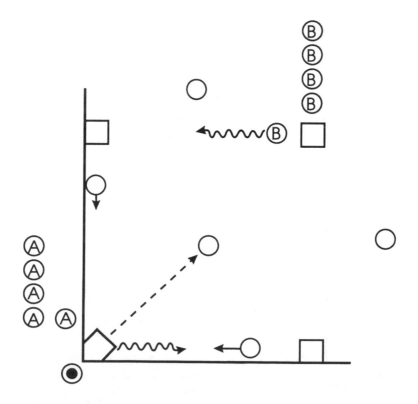

11

SPECIAL CATEGORY DRILLS

Double Steal Defense

196 DOUBLE STEAL DEFENSE - BASERUNNERS AT FIRST AND THIRD

Objective: To have the catcher practice looking at a baserunner who is on third base, trying to freeze him, and then throwing out the baserunner from first base who is attempting to steal second base.

Equipment Needed: Full catching gear, bases, baseballs, and gloves.

Description: The drill involves four players: two baserunners (one at first base [C] and one on third base[D]) and two catchers (one positioned behind the plate as a receiver [A] and one serving as a middle infielder [B] to cover second base). The drill begins by having player A feign receiving a pitch. With a ball in his hand, player A then looks at third, freezes the runner, and fires the ball to B at second base to throw out the baserunner from first base who is attempting to steal second. After a preset number of plays, the players rotate positions.

Coaching Points:

- The drill can be performed without a ball (phantom style) in order to save stress on player A's arm. Everyone just goes through the proper motions - no ball is actually thrown.

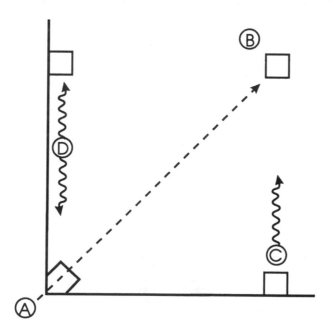

197 DOUBLE STEAL DEFENSE - BASERUNNERS AT FIRST AND THIRD, THROW TO HOME

Objective: To have the second baseman practice the techniques involved in serving as the relay man while defending against the double steal situation with baserunners on first base and third base.

Equipment Needed: Full catching gear, bases, baseballs, and gloves.

Description: The drill involves four players: two baserunners (one at first base [A] and one on third base [B]), a catcher, and a second baseman (C). The drill begins by having the catcher feign receiving a pitch and announcing, "Go." At that point, the baserunner who was on first base starts for second base which is covered by the second baseman. The catcher then throws the ball to the second baseman. Simultaneously, the baserunner on third breaks for home. The second baseman then throws the ball back to the catcher in an attempt to get the runner coming home from third base. If the third baseman sees the baserunner on third break for home, he yells, "Home." On the other hand, if the second baseman feels that the baserunner at third base has wandered too far from the bag, he can throw directly to third in an attempt to catch the baserunner off the bag before he can safely get back.

Coaching Points:

- The drill can be performed without a ball (phantom style) in order to minimize any strain on the catcher's arm. Each player involved in the drill just goes through the motions - no ball is actually thrown.

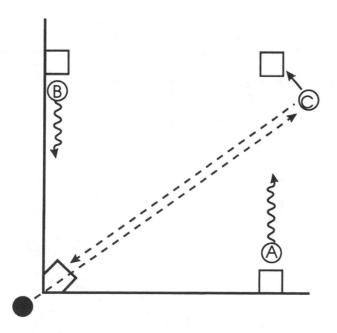

198 DOUBLE STEAL DEFENSE: BASERUNNERS AT FIRST AND THIRD - CUTOFF THROW TO HOME

Objective: To practice the cutoff throw-to-home special play for defending against the possible first and third double steal.

Equipment Needed: Full catching gear, bases, baseballs, and gloves.

Description: The drill involves five players: two baserunners (one at first base [A] and one at third base [B]), a catcher, and two middle infielders (a shortstop [C] and a second baseman [D]). With the double steal a possibility, the catcher signals to the middle infielders that he wants to put on a special double steal defensive play. If a right-handed hitter is in the batter's box, the catcher will fire the ball out to the second baseman, who will race in from his normal position to the lip of the infield grass to catch the throw from the catcher. Even though a baserunner is breaking for second, the second baseman does not go toward second base at all. The catcher goes through his normal first and third check points, looks to third base, and then fires the ball directly to the second baseman. Hopefully, the baserunner at third base will see the ball go past the pitcher's mound and fail to notice the change in the defensive alignment for receiving the throw. If the baserunner on third base then breaks for home, he should be an easy out on the return throw from the second baseman to the catcher. If a left-handed hitter is at the plate, the same procedures should take place, except that the catcher's throw is now directed to the shortstop who has also assumed a drawn-in position on the lip of the infield grass.

Coaching Points:

- The drill can be performed without a ball (phantom style) in order to minimize any strain on the catcher's arm. Each player involved in the drill just goes through the motions - no ball is actually thrown.
- The defense must become the aggressor in baserunners-on-first-and-third, double-steal situations.
- First-and-third, double-steal situations demand a lot of practice time to master properly.

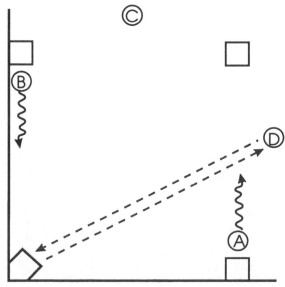

199 DOUBLE STEAL DEFENSE: BASERUNNERS AT FIRST AND THIRD, READ AND THROW

Objective: To practice reading the situation with baserunners at first base and on third base in a double steal situation and making an appropriate throw.

Equipment Needed: Full catching gear, bases, baseballs, and gloves.

Description: The drill involves six players: two baserunners (one at first base [A]and one at third base [B]), a catcher, a third baseman (C), a middle infielder (D), and a pitcher (E). The drill begins by having the pitcher from a shortened distance (approximately 30 to 40 feet away) throw a pitch to the catcher. The catcher initially attempts to freeze the baserunner at third base by looking at him. The catcher is actually reading his own third baseman. If the third baseman feels that the baserunner on third has gone too far down the line, he throws both of his hands in the air and moves to a position approximately three feet inside the baseline, parallel with the third base bag. Anytime the catcher sees the third baseman's hands raised, he then throws to the inside of the base (trying not to hit the baserunner in the back) to the third baseman who attempts to make the tag play on the baserunner who is scrambling back to the bag. The catcher can throw directly to third without first faking a throw to second base, or he can fake a throw to second base, take a short crow hop, and then fire the ball to third base.

Coaching Points:

- The drill can be performed without a ball (phantom style) in order to minimize any strain on the catcher's arm. Each player involved in the drill just goes through the motions - no ball is actually thrown.
- The defense must become the aggressor in baserunners-on-first-and-third, double-steal situations.
- First and third, double steal situations demand a lot of practice time to master properly.

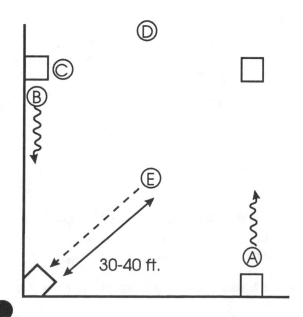

30-40 ft.

BATTER UP WITH MASTERS PRESS!

YOU CAN TEACH HITTING

Dusty Baker, Jeff Mercer, and Marv Bittinger

More than a set of instructions and guidelines for swinging a bat, *You Can Teach Hitting* takes you from selecting your bat to selecting your pitch, from the science of the swing to the art of situational hitting. Lavishly illustrated with full color phototographs and stunning computer graphics, *You Can Teach Hitting* is truly a one-of-a-kind book.

> 256 pages • 8 ½ x 9 ⅛
> 0-940279-73-8 • $24.95
> color photos throughout
> paper

BASEBALL CROSSWORDS

Mark Roszkowski

A fun new way for baseball fans of all ages to enjoy their favorite sport! Each chapter includes a condensed history of a major league team, key statistics, and a crossword puzzle with clues to test your knowledge of that team's history and players.

> 160 pages • 7 x 10
> 0-940279-55-X • $12.95
> puzzles and graphs
> paper

YOUTH LEAGUE BASEBALL

Skip Bertman

A terrific guide for coaches and parents! With a chapter devoted to each specific phase of the game, this book covers all the positions. Basic skills such as throwing and catching as well as more complex matters such as position fundamentals are all addressed in an easily comprehensible manner. Includes a fault correction index to help coaches find the information they need as quickly as possible.

> 192 pages • 5¼ x 8 ¼
> 0-940279-68-1 • $9.95
> b/w photos
> paper

All Masters Press books, including those in the Spalding Sports Library, are available in bookstores nationwide or directly from the publisher by calling (800) 722-2677.

Call now for your free catalog of sports books!

MASTERS PRESS

DEAR VALUED CUSTOMER,

Masters Press is dedicated to bringing you timely and authoritative books for your personal and professional library. As a leading publisher of sports and fitness books, our goal is to provide you with easily accessible information on topics that interest you written by the most qualified authors. You can assist us in this endeavor by checking the box next to your particular areas of interest.

We appreciate your comments and will use the information to provide you with an expanded and more comprehensive selection of titles.

Thank you very much for taking the time to provide us with this helpful information.

Cordially,
Masters Press

Areas of interest in which you'd like to see Masters Press publish books:

☐ COACHING BOOKS
   Which sports? What level of competition?

☐ INSTRUCTIONAL/DRILL BOOKS
   Which sports? What level of competition?

☐ FITNESS/EXERCISE BOOKS
   ☐ Strength—Weight Training
   ☐ Body Building
   ☐ Other

☐ REFERENCE BOOKS
   what kinds?

☐ BOOKS ON OTHER
   Games, Hobbies
   or Activities

Are you more likely to read a book or watch a video-tape to get the sports information you are looking for?

I'm interested in the following sports as a participant:

I'm interested in the following sports as an observer:

Please feel free to offer any comments or suggestions to help us shape our publishing plan for the future.

Name _____ Age _____

Address _____

City _____ State _____ Zip _____

Daytime phone number _____

BUSINESS REPLY MAIL

FIRST CLASS MAIL   PERMIT NO. 1317   INDIANAPOLIS IN

POSTAGE WILL BE PAID BY ADDRESSEE

MASTERS PRESS

2647 WATERFRONT PKY EAST DR

INDIANAPOLIS IN 46209-1418